THE MORE YOU HATE ME

Andy Smart

For information contact:
Unsolicited Press
Portland, Oregon
www.unsolicitedpress.com
orders@unsolicitedpress.com
619-354-8005

Cover Design: Kathryn Gerhardt
Editor: Gage Greenspan and S.R. Stewart

ISBN: 978-1-956692-27-3

I would like to extend my thanks to the following individuals:

Anne-Marie Oomen, for your mentorship, immense patience, and friendship; Lisa Allen, for your editorial and personal support; Ashley Johnson, for being the little homie and all that entails; Jennifer Grant, for your support both logistical and spiritual; Randall Horton, for helping me keep the faith; Chief Mark Jednaszewski, for being my brother on the page and off of it; Chris McCarthy, for always being there; and my mother, Jan, for everything.

I would also like to thank the editors of *Moon City Review*, where the essay "A Numbers Game" originally appeared, in a slightly different form.

For Mom.

And Dad.

THE MORE YOU HATE ME

INTRODUCTION

This book is not a love song for my father; that will be obvious fairly quickly. It is also not devoted to the praise of *Full Metal Jacket* as either a cinematic work or an artifact of sentimental relevance. This book, and the version of myself presented therein, is often brash and abrasive. In this book, I show and I tell. I give away hard truths about my father, my mother, my life. And I am pervasively and undeniably my old man's kid. I often revert to a riff on the verbiage and tone of Stanley Kubrick's characters and (as a result of his obsession with the film) the lingua franca of my father. The title of this book comes from Gunnery Sergeant Hartman's opening monolog.

The Gunny prophecies that because he's a hard man the recruits will hate his guts. But, he says, that hatred will make him a better instructor.

Of all the words from *Full Metal Jacket* which carom around in my mind on any given day, these are the most relevant now. When I hate my father most is when his ghost gives me an epiphany. When I hate the film most is when I realize, once more, how much I have needed it before. When you hate me most, read closely. I can be hard. But I'm fair.

Andy Smart

EASIER FORGIVENESS

"It's easier to get forgiveness than permission," an old, hackneyed proverb says. While it may be true for some, perhaps most, situations, the author of the aphorism never dealt with Warner Bros. Entertainment, owner of the film *Full Metal Jacket*. When I approached the film giant about this project, informing them of my father's suicide and its eerie similarity to events in Kubrick's masterpiece, they responded with a shadowy denial. "Confidential contractual" issues prevented them from allowing me to quote the film or its script directly. Character's names and summaries of events are fair use, but the language—the lexicon of hard speech I grew up around—was off limits.

Bear this in mind as you move through the book: in most cases where I originally quoted the film, I was really quoting my father. It pains me not to be allowed to do so here. However, where doing something without permission generally doesn't result in serious consequences: I can't afford to be sued. It's funny, though. Marines can't die, Hartman says, unless they get permission. My old man died without permission and I still haven't forgiven him all the way.

Even in the small defeat of playing by Warner Bros.' rules, I'm evolving. The book is evolving. In the paraphrasing and approximation of dialogue, reader, I hope you'll begin to see me—I've rotated back to the world and I'm moving in it. Being forced to leave the film's exactitudes may be a blessing.

Moving on.

PRAY

This is the Rifleman's Creed, as recited in *Full Metal Jacket*. It is also a network of experiential fragments in disguise. These are the vignettes which follow.

This is my rifle.

There are many like it, but this one is mine.

My rifle is my best friend.

It is my life.

I must master it as I must master my life.

Without me, my rifle is useless. Without my rifle, I am useless.

I must fire my rifle true.

I must shoot straighter than my enemy, who is trying to kill me. I must shoot him before he shoots me.

I will.

Before God I swear this creed.

My rifle and myself are the defenders of my country.

We are the masters of our enemy.

We are the saviors of my life.

So be it.

Until there is no enemy, but peace.

Amen.

PRAY

This is MY . . .

The problem begins here: *My.*

Dad's guns were almost all new, out-of-the-box, with the only middleman being the retailer. But the gun he used to kill himself was a preowned Smith and Wesson revolver my mother bought from a now-defunct pawn shop (it's the St. Louis Turkish Society, at the time of this entry).

It was Dad's; but it was someone else's first—the barrel was already christened by another man's hollow-points or target loads; the gun had lain under that man's pillow or in his nightstand drawer, a Linus blanket against the specter of home invasion; it had killed a squirrel or blown liquor bottles to smithereens on the outskirts of a bootheel Missouri farm. A boy had tried and failed to earn his father's approval by squeezing the trigger and wincing against the recoil.

My old man's inherited .38 witnessed emotions effable only through the weapon's report.

And then the gun was hocked. I've played with all the possible reasons why. Every storyline about what separated that weapon from its owner: an accidental close call that left a child in tears, a father red-faced, and a mother resolute that there would be no more guns in her home? An overdue gas bill that was just covered by the underbid value of the family firearm? Trading it toward a higher caliber with more stopping power and a rail for mounting a laser sight? Or a simple "fuck it, who needs this thing around"?

This, along with a cache of other histories, I will never know for sure.

It was party to the everyday atrocities of being and unbecoming.

. . . RIFLE.

If it is Christmas, 1974 this would be true. Mom gave Dad a Winchester .22 with a 5X40 Bushnell scope as an "Our First Married Christmas" gift. Her grandmother, my great-grandma Pauline, who gave me half of my middle name, bought Dad a case for that rifle. It was an off-white canvas with a hard leather top, tooled cowhide bottom quarter, and an adjustable strap. It's a little worn now, but it still looks more like art than armament; I should know, it's under my bed. Pop's rifle, too, of course. I take it out and fiddle with it sometimes, usually when I'm drunk and feeling that queer, liminal sensation that straddles nostalgia and morbidity. By now the firing pin would need replacing. I consider taking it to a sporting goods megastore or even a gunsmith. Getting it cleaned, replacing the pin and maybe the barrel, but never the stock—one monument to the weapon's age and resilience, replete with nicks and gouges.

But why? Do I need to resurrect the dead? And is that the way to do it?

Moreover, if we fast forward to the spring of 1980, the word rifle is at best imprecise; by that time, Dad had a small arsenal—enough artillery to make him feel like one of the mercenaries in *Soldier of Fortune* or a step-cousin of the folks from Ruby Ridge. They ate up   a lot of closet space too. Probably the crown jewel of the old man's collection, though, was the self-appointed "Combat Magnum," officially known as the Colt Python .357. Dad's was a six-inch, which he swore (according to Mom; I wasn't born yet) didn't dampen the recoil as much as he'd expected. The four-inch would've acted as a concealed-carry cannon or been tucked under the front seat of his Nova. Nonetheless, it was (and remains, among gun buffs and historians) one of the finest revolvers ever mass-produced. For a few dollars more and a few extra ounces of weight, Dad could've had the Dirty Harry elephant gun: Smith and Wesson's M29 .44 Magnum with an eight-and-a-half-inch barrel; why he settled, I don't know.

Mom made Dad sell the Colt, along with his pistol-grip .20-gauge Mossberg shotgun and the Springfield Armory 1911, plus the remainder, whose names and specs have gotten lost in the ether of time when she got pregnant with me. They'd been married for ten years and were finally with child. It was all my mother ever wanted: a baby. No amount of trigger locks could change her mind. Zero guns in the house until I was much older.

So began my father's slavery, as he'd call it later. The long years of emasculation by way of forfeiting firepower.

THERE ARE MANY LIKE IT . . .

For the old man's fiftieth birthday, Mom and I went halves on a shotgun—*the* shotgun, by a lot of standards. Remington's Model 870 Express, the youngest and most affordable installment of the original 870 Wingmaster. Express came in .12 and .20 gauge; we went with the .12, plus an extended magazine and a twenty-eight-inch supermag barrel to accommodate ballsier ammunition. Its aesthetic was simple and clean, classic: matte blue receiver (which looks black, I don't care what the catalog says) and a rich, warm, hardwood pump and butt. The only nod to extra comfort was a rubber cap on the butt to protect the shooter's shoulder. It came in a cardboard box with the image of the weapon's grandfather model screened on the lid.

I was twenty-one—had just become old enough to buy my own beer. There was a strange exhilaration in buying a gun, even if it wasn't my own. Over a decade later, I've decided it's the awesome realization that a person can put that much responsibility in the hands of another. I gave my father what the American Society for Suicide Prevention calls "lethal means." It's a contributing factor in a large percentage of suicides. I put the decision to fire outward or inward in my father's hands, trusting him to make the right call. When he died, he put the yoke of living or dying on my shoulders, an old rucksack for a new soldier. Having marched, as I have, into my thirties and through some emotional jungles (though I'm still hacking through life, sometimes blindly), I can see a wanting in my younger self. A wanting to be like my dad. I can't explain it now and I would've denied it then. But it was there.

That was two years before Dad died: February of 2005. By 2009, the different iterations of the 870 had sold over ten million units. (Isn't that a cozy way to think of lethal implements?) Its mammoth commercial popularity was enough for at least one online gun forum to call the 870 "the finest shotgun ever made."

Our family contributed one more unit to the 870's overall infamy. Not to be outdone, Dad bought me a piece of my own for my twenty-first birthday the following summer, though he opted for a faux-tactical, black-on-black job.

"You kids like to look cool instead of just gettin' the job done," he said. "Form over function. All show."

"Didn't stop you from blowin' a couple hundred bucks on it, did it?" I asked.

"One day your mouth is gonna write a check your ass can't cover."

"Runs in the family."

. . . but this one is MINE.

Behold, the ticklish topic of ownership comes up again.

The day Dad got that shotgun, he ugly-cried; the tired skin under his grey eyes collected rivulets of tears that would, once every few seconds, dribble into the big, wet river of sentiment flowing south from cheeks to jowls. His glasses were on the kitchen table in front of him—brown frames with no tortoise shell or any pattern at all, Coke-bottle-thick lenses with dandruff and dead skin flecked around the edges, and clear demarcations for the bifocal. Mom and I stood there, dumbstruck and a little embarrassed.

"Jeff," Mom hazarded, "do you like it?"

Stupid questions can often jar loose some dialogue. We were counting on that.

"I love it," Pop said. His voice was creeping toward a falsetto, something totally mismatched to his body and the gun across his lap. Slowly, he sat the weapon upright on his knee and opened and closed the ejection port. He looked at me, or in my direction (he was legally blind by age twelve). "Free men own weapons. Slaves don't." I could hear the phlegm in his throat.

"I'm glad you like it, Dad." What else do you say to that? I fumbled a cigarette around in my pocket, wondering if I could sneak outside and smoke. It was the first time I saw Dad as a drama queen. "I'm gonna take the trash out," I said.

I came back seven minutes later, smelling of Marlboro Reds and Tommy Hilfiger cologne. Dad was field stripping the Remington while Mom powerwalked on her treadmill. My grandmother was dying, almost forgotten, in the back bedroom. My dog Buddy was chewing on his hindquarters.

Ennui in the barracks. The intricate and arrogant ballet around the elephant in the room.

*

Pop never put a single shell through that weapon, instead leaving it to collect dust and look more sad than menacing. After the first week, he didn't clean it anymore. It's funny, thinking about the decays our eyes can't perceive. I'm sure there was oil buildup in the barrel, the sights were out of whack, the trigger pull was loosening and making the weapon imprecise, all manner of things.

We parted with that shotgun forever on June 15, 2007, the same day we parted with Sergeant Dad. My buddy Bradley came by the house in response to my frantic phone call.

"I need you to do me a favor. Big one, and quick as you can," I said.

"Alright, man. What up?" He'd only lived in Missouri a year, not long enough to cure his Kentucky drawl.

"My dad shot himself out on the patio this morning, man. Blew himself to hell. He's gone. Mom's freaked and she wants all the guns out. Cops are all over the fucking place and they won't even let me pick anything up to make sure it's not loaded. He used the .38. They're keeping it as evidence or some shit. But I've got everything else here."

"Jesus . . . give me fifteen, I gotta get the dogs loaded up." He and his girlfriend had just adopted a Jack Russel and taken in Bradley's mother's Doberman mix. This particular morning, Bradley was alone with the pups.

"Okay. Thank you, B."

I waited on the front porch, wishing I had a smoke. Neighbors were beginning to drive past, gawking at the crime scene tape draped across our open back gate and the ambulances and coroner's cars half-parked on our lawn. It was brutal hot out that day, pushing a hundred at 0930. Bradley's Jeep pulled up as an Italian police sergeant, Carmelo, was walking out to ask if I had a shovel in my garage.

"There's a bit of a mess back there, as you can imagine," he said. "We'll try to make it as unobtrusive as we can, but—"

"Hey, brother," Bradley said, long-striding up the steps. "Fuck me, I'm sorry."

He and Carmelo shook hands.

"Give this guy your guns," Carmelo said to me. "Give him your garage keys too." He took Bradley's elbow. "Come with me."

A part of me wants to know, but the majority has enjoyed the ignorance of knowing what happened during the cleanup phase that morning. All I know is the next time I saw Bradley he was pale and his hands were shaking.

"Did you see?" he asked.

"No. Just from way back, him lying there. He had his hands under his head, it looked like. It was really like he was sleeping."

"Never stop thinking that. Let's get those gats in the car."

He took custody of Dad's shotgun and mine, plus the old man's .22 and my Ruger .9mm.

"I'll try to get these back from you as soon as I can, man," I said.

"No hurry, I got plenty of space. Might take that pistol for a spin, though." Was he trying to make me smile? Was he conscious of how close to breaking I was, standing in the sun with my life in shambles behind me? Or was that just Bradley making chitchat with his friend? I don't care, I don't think.

"Do it, it's a great gun."

"Nah, brother. That'd be like you doing stuff with my girl. Just isn't right."

"Well then, buddy, you better put a whole lot of bullets through that pistol there, 'cause me and Elaine . . ."

"Alright, ass, I'm giving you that one on account of you're having a bad day."

"Really, B, thank you."

"Don't mention it."

For a year afterward, we didn't. Then, after some intense cajoling, Mom reversed her stance and began allowing me to bring the munitions home.

"But nothing is loaded and I keep the bullets," she said.

"How in the hell am I supposed to protect us from anything with an unloaded gun, Ma?"

"Your shotgun doubles as a boat oar or a billyclub, and your pistol is like big brass knuckles."

I had no chance of winning any more ground than I had, and we both knew it. There was, however, one point I could negotiate.

"I was thinking Brad could keep Dad's twelve gauge."

"Okay," Mom said. Her voice was neither thin nor far-off. For a woman in a pink nightgown, she was damn firm.

"You're sure? You don't care?"

"I gave it to him, he left it to you whether he meant to or not, and if you want to give it to Brad, that's fine. He's a good boy, and you tell him I say so."

*

Brad was touched by the gesture. He made sure to keep me apprised of where the gun was and what it was doing, such as when, a couple of hunting seasons after he became the weapon's owner, it killed a doe on the second-to-last-day to bag deer.

He texted me a picture of the carcass, skinned and dripping blood in the basement of his apartment building. It was captioned "Landlord is gonna shit if we don't get this little lady butchered PDQ! Thanks for the shotty. She did great!"

Only in later years, over bourbon and after Brad became a father himself, would he confide in me how horrible it was, the killing.

"Had to track her for a long way, man. First shot hipped her, second one missed, third one got her in the foreleg or something. She must've laid in the leaves waiting for the last one for an hour."

The last one went through the heart at close range. If you looked at the hide, Brad said, you could see the scorch circle where the muzzle flash had burned the doe's fur.

"Damn, son," I said.

We were quiet awhile, only speaking with our eyes and our clinking ice cubes.

"I think I'm going to get one of them shell holsters for the side of the stock," Brad said.

"Those are badass. You always see 'em in movies when the SWAT team rolls up."

"Hell yeah. I'm gonna be hardcore. Like Rambo. Only, you know, not buff or runnin' around shooting at Brian Dennehy."

"Might as well join the NRA. Get yourself a discount on merch and maybe a picture with Charlton Heston. Old Moses is gonna die soon, better get it while it's good."

We carried on that way, happier all the time to have moved back into fictional violence and the coziness of bullshit bravado. We're still carrying on, in truth.

Brad showed me another picture of the gun the other day at work, all kitted out with accoutrements.

"Fancy," I said, gesturing like I might faint.

"That's not your papa's shotgun, buddy,"," Brad said.

We both saw—and regretted—the parallel to Hartman and Cowboy in FMJ. Truth is thoughtless like that, fucking up a tender moment and a joke all at once.

"Nope, sure isn't."

There was nothing else to say.

My rifle is my **BEST FRIEND**.

Mom and I were standing on the curb outside the Scottrade Center after a bull ride. We were into that for a couple of years, and the Pro Bull Riders came through St. Louis in February of each of those years. During that time I started calling my mother Madre, and I'd sometimes refer to myself in the third person as Cowboy. Dad was still Dad, or Pop, never Paco or Padre, and damn sure never Amigo. Whatever we called him, my father was always our ride to those events. Pop dropped us off and was our chauffeur-in-waiting until we were ready to come home.

It was cold and Madre was only four days outside the worst of a case of walking pneumonia, meaning she probably shouldn't have come. Hindsight. But she did come, and there was another night of action remaining. She was anxious to stop tempting fate and retreat indoors. The venue forbade reentry. Once we went out, we were out.

We waited, watching traffic and our breath.

I called Dad. Called again. And again. I could fabricate a total amount of unanswered phone calls in the interest of dramatic flourish, but I can only think to say I called every several seconds for twenty minutes and then finally called a cab. In St. Louis, taxis are not a simple thing to procure, especially not in 2006 or 7. In total, Madre and I waited almost an hour, paid twenty-five dollars, and walked into our house to find Dad passed out on the sofa, sitting with his phone on one knee and his pistol on the other. His gut was flumped over a belt buckle with his first name on it, dandruff was caked around the stretched-out neck of his black t-shirt, his work boots were laced loose for easy slipping-on when Go Time came. The TV was playing the end credits to *Full Metal Jacket*, and there were cotton swabs and paper towels strewn on the cushion next to the sleeping man's ass.

"Hey, jerkoff," I shout. No response.

"Thanks for the ride, great provider, wonderful husband," Mom says, in a louder-than-normal voice. Again the old man is unmoved. Mom goes to kick his shins. I turn off the TV as I stomp toward the kitchen in my cowboy boots.

I don't hear my father bolt awake. Instead, through a cloud of grog and "oh fuck," I hear: "Goddamn it Janet, I'm sorry, I was cleaning gunk out of the cylinders and watching a movie waiting for you to call. I've already logged sixty hours at work this week and I'll pay the boy back for the fucking cab. Where is the boy, anyway?"

Madre's voice gets tinny when she's that angry, like the blades of a blender chewing up a beer can and wheezing out a cloud of shrapnel. Her words aren't important; I know the gist from other battles.

"I get it, woman, I said I'm fucking sorry. The boy works, too. He had enough to get you back. I'll reimburse him and we'll be square. I failed; I get it. That's what I do. You're never too shy to let me know about it. Believe me, I'm aware. Now where is the boy?"

I am over being nameless in my father's lexicon. I am over being a biological circumstance. I am drunk and I am pissed and there is one more beer in the fridge and I'm drinking it as I reenter the fray of the living room.

"Andrew. I have a name, you fat putz."

"Watch your mouth. I'm still your father."

"And that isn't my fault. Mom was kind enough to breed with you and here I be."

"Who exactly do you think you are, boy?"

"I'm nobody's boy, that's for starters. And I think I'm the one who had to pick up after you when you shirked your commitment to be there for your wife and child. That's who I am. Ain't much thinking to do about it. But you knew that already, didn't you, Dad? That thinking is overrated?"

Toward the end of the opening act of *Full Metal Jacket,* Joker narrates that the drill instructors are proud of the recruits for growing beyond their control. My father was less proud of me. I could see it in the straight-backed, jaw-locked, still-wrong-but-always-fighting posture in which he lingered on the sofa.

"Son, I'm not going to sit here and say you don't have the right to be angry, but you're out of line. Respect will be paid while you live in my house."

What stopped the next words from coming, kept me from emancipating myself and going off Huck Finn style down the wild river toward a new story to tell? Not the logistics of taking on all the bills I still didn't pay myself: phone, car, health insurance, rent. It wasn't the fear of hearing the old man sigh with relief when I packed my shit and left, or the indifference of the big bad world toward where, or if, I lived.

It was my mother standing at the vertex of the angle between me and the door, stranded. She was unemployed and unemployable. She was Dad's prisoner and I couldn't replace his wardenship, but I could stay. It's not in *FMJ* but it's one of the oldest soldiering tropes of them all: Leave no one behind.

I was twirling my invisible rifle on a drill team of shadows and impending regrets and I was damn good at it.

Snap to attention.

"Sir, yes sir."

It is MY LIFE.

We've seen the power of gun mythos over my father; we've seen how he wished that sway to be hereditary; we've seen a man whose identity and essence are parts of a firearm. But it is not enough to know how my father adored The Weapon, for this is only obvious, myopic.

Dad would agree that The Weapon was his life because of its defensive capabilities—its surety of laying down any man who assailed the castle while my old man sat on the throne. *Dicto Simplicitur,* all that.

But the Weapon was truly Dad's life because of its ultimate stopping power—its gorgeous gift of an emergency exit. My father's life was not in how it was lived, but in how it ended.

The Weapon was always the endgame. I know this now, too late.

I must MASTER IT.

I was ten years old in the summer of 1994, about to turn eleven. It was the first year of my life there would be no World Series; Major League Baseball was in the throes of a player strike. It was a jading time for me. In retrospect, it was one of those *Wonder Years*-ish moments that only became a rite of passage later on. I remember crying to my mother that it wasn't fair.

"Shh," she cooed. "It'll be alright. It can't last forever." She smelled, always, of vanilla perfume from Target and the decaf coffee she drank because the real stuff gave her panic attacks.

My father had a different reaction altogether. Instead of sympathy, and certainly in favor of babying me, he enlisted a sly, self-serving agenda. He bought me a black, pneumatic pump Daisy air rifle for my eleventh birthday. He bought a plastic target holder and BB catcher too, plus some fancy, yellowed shooting glasses. He fashioned a bench rest out of an old end table and, *viola,* we had a basement shooting range.

"Forget about baseball, boy," Dad said. "You're a man, now. A young man, but a man all the same. No more games. You think Ozzie Smith or Cal Ripken are going to swoop in with a ball bat and protect this house? Bullshit. You take this weapon here. Even if you never have to use it on anybody, it's fun. Come on."

He showed me how to pump air into the gun, careful to point it downrange and never pump too many times. Six times, max.

"Now sight up," he said. His mechanic's hands molded my own onto the trigger guard and pump. "Breathe, goddammit. Relax."

Dad slapped my neck and reminded me this was serious shit. He told me to take half a breath in, let it halfway out, and then squeeze the trigger. I tried to do the fractional breathing right but failed. I jerked up when the trigger came back sent a brass BB caroming off the limestone wall behind the target.

"Nerves. We all get 'em," Dad said. It was gentler than I thought it'd be. Mistakes weren't a thing he dealt with patiently. "Now settle the fuck down and go again."

I can't remember how long we stayed there, but it went until I was crying and tired and had long since wanted to quit. I was plugging rounds through the outer rings of the target reliably, but Sergeant Dad would only settle for a bullseye.

"You will qualify expert on this weapon, son. You have to, or how am I supposed to get you behind something with some gonads?"

That was it. This was his segue into the second coming of his cache of weaponry. I was going to be his excuse. It was one thing to object in my head, another to put words in the air. Dad knew it, too.

"You'd like that, wouldn't you? Your own weapon? And not this pussy shit, either. I know I told you it wasn't a toy, but it is compared to what you could have. You want to graduate, don't you?"

I squinted into the glare of the old fluorescent bulbs and the lone halogen lamp beside the bench rest.

"Yes, sir," I said.

Dad had paced off twenty yards to a drywall façade, an open alcove where old power tools and computer equipment laid dead or dying, melted into a narrow chute.

If I sent a round straight down, hit the ten ring, then it would all be over, at least for the moment. I sucked in dry air and held it, feeling the mildew coating my throat. I fired.

Just outside the center, the target tore.

"Nice," Dad said. "Almost there."

"I can't do it anymore. My eyes are tired and my finger hurts."

"Fine. Quit. Be a fuckin quitter."

"I'm not a quitter."

"What did you say?"

"I said I'm not a quitter. It's my first time."

"Sir. 'It's my first time, sir.' Don't forget yourself with me, boy."

"Yes, sir."

"Now quit. Your mother always wanted a daughter anyway."

We were the remnant of a platoon dispatched from who knows where. Mom was the Lieutenant, calling the shots even if it seemed otherwise. Dad was the combat veteran squad leader, bucking orders and advancing on bush know-how, ambition, and the requisite amount of schoolboy bully mentality. I was a puke: too young to be a grunt, too stupid and malleable. The gun in my hand was my weapon against paper circles and pop cans; I was my father's weapon against my mother; fear was his weapon against me.

Dad was a sniper of the psyche. I knew I had better fall in and square myself away; I could run to *mama san*, but there was no camo on earth that could get me out of the old soldier's sights. Especially when I counted on him to drop me off at Hope Lutheran School, where I tried to learn about the Civil War without dozing off, bored because I'd been there and was going back. I was a boy for a few hours that year. For the rest of the time, I was a combat correspondent with vocal chords made of glass.

This is to say I was screaming in a voice that was cracking, slowly becoming audible over the battle cries of my upbringing. A scream might've helped, but only if it were mine. Too many others hung thick in the air and ricocheted off the walls; people wounding one another with the same friendly fire over and over again.

We carried ourselves as a household for decades, until a history of dropping napalm on our own camp came to a head. We weren't playing war, but we weren't waging it either. That was my father's contribution: a violence structured so it was totally unrecognizable. Sun Tzu, eat your heart out. Pop had

Mom and I conditioned to believe our family was normal. Married people fight; sons hate their fathers; Men rule the roost; to the victor goes the spoils. Nobody wins a game like that, and it isn't very much fun.

Pop and I went to two baseball games a year, even after he'd told me to forget it. I always got straight A's and the local paper had partnered with the St. Louis Cardinals to award four tickets to every kid with perfect grades.

The last game I remember was against the Pittsburgh Pirates. By the sixth inning, the Cardinals were losing 9-0.

"You about ready, big guy?" Dad asked. "You've got school tomorrow."

"It's Friday, Dad. And besides, the game's not over."

"Well it might be Friday, but this game is history. You got heart, son, but you're lying to yourself."

"Two grand slams and a two-run homer and we win. It could happen. Anything can happen."

Anything can happen. I still believe that, about life and baseball.

*

Somehow I still remember the Atlanta Braves winning the Series in 1995. Dad was out of town for work and I didn't miss an inning. I sat, if you can call it that, in a bean bag on the living room floor, bouncing a tennis ball off the baseboard next to the TV stand and into my ball glove. Pre-smartphones, it was a lot less antagonistic than present day, but Mark Wohlers was still my bazooka and my middle finger on the night of Game Six. I was too young to have the first, too quick to use the latter.

It was perfect.

Pop was at least pretending to root against the Braves so we'd have some rivalry, even in an arena he looked down on. But even if the Braves lost, I could still go back and see how it happened: a hung fastball, a picked-off baserunner. Bad luck, jet lag, a curse of some kind. I understood baseball, thought of it as pure. Even when it hurt your feelings, it was still a beautiful thing. There was always, as my old man used to teach me, Next Season. It's not so in other games or anti-games, or in war, be it public or private. It's not.

. . . as I must MASTER MY LIFE.

Schopenhauer writes: "there is nothing in the world to which each male has a more unassailable title than to his own life and person."

Pop never read that, I'm sure, because it never graced the pages of a Tom Clancy novel or the *Time Life* pictorial history of the Vietnam War, but somehow he shared this philosophy—that a man (not a woman; my father was born in the 50's and survived the 60's as a square who hoped and prayed for the permanence of patriarchy) was blessed with the innate privilege of controlling his own fate. If the bank were asking for a mortgage payment Dad couldn't make, he just . .

. didn't make it. And when he owed a dental bill for my braces in eighth grade, he kept on owing it until the third collection agency threatened to garnish his wages, just to prove to himself he hadn't been mastered by his debt.

We lived outside our means in every way we could manage. My birthday celebration was longer than Hanukkah, Christmas was bigger than my birthday, and no kid in Missouri had a swankier tooth fairy than I did. (Twenty bucks and some Topp's baseball cards for a molar, but there was no Ken Griffey Jr. in the pack, so it could've been better.) But we were poor and Dad knew it. Or, as he used to tell me:

"We're broke. Poor is worse." To compensate for a lifetime's worth of mismanaged funds, Pop knew, to the last decimal place, how much he was worth in life insurance.

"First thing, Janet," he'd say to Mom, "if anything ever happens to me, you pay off this house."

She would shush him, if she were feeling tender. Often she was not and would instead throw him a verbal beating along the lines of, "You know I hate when you talk like that! Why would you do that? It makes my anxieties flare! Why are you always so morbid? Why do you do this to me?"

Something like that.

"Because sooner or later, I'm going to die," he'd say.

"What if I die first?"

Dad would kiss Mom's forehead knowingly.

"You won't."

WITHOUT ME, MY RIFLE IS USELESS. WITH MY RIFLE, I AM USELESS.

A weapon sits alone on a nightstand, waiting. The sleeping man who owns it snores and starts, his sleep apnea and obesity warring on his body and brain at once. The sleeping man is my father, of course, but without his weapon he is only one unconscious human, nothing more. He is not a father in his sleep, nor a husband, a soldier, a mechanic, a football fan, or someone who eats corn chips dunked in mayonnaise. Nothing—he accomplishes and represents nothing. Likewise, the weapon. It's not rescuing or protecting. It, too, is sleeping and devoid of value. When the sleeping man wakes, his hand will grope for his glasses and his gun. His mouth will be dry, his eyelids heavy, his boots and pants and work shirt where he left them. He will leave them, lay and sit naked on the edge of the bed holding his weapon and scratching his balls.

In the thimbleful of time they have together, my old man and his sidearm are as precious as they'll be.

In the extended version of the Rifleman's Creed, as it appears in Gustav Hasford's *The Short-Timers*, on which FMJ is based, there is a line my father never read or heard:

"My Rifle is human, even as I, because it is my life."

Here my father believed the creed but belied reality. He used to tell me he was worth more dead than alive. To him, what counted was the tangible. Something with weight and purpose, like the gun. To the gun, my father mattered because:

"In war it is . . . the hits that count. We will hit."

Dad had at least one brother he loved. He loved its sights, barrel, and trigger. He pitied its lack of blood, so he gave it his own. They would both go down together.

*

Pop only threatened suicide once. He'd drained ten thousand dollars from his and Mom's checking account and couldn't tell anybody how.

"I don't know," he kept stammering. Mom and I were livid, both screaming. I was twenty-one.

"How could you do this to her?" I demanded. I was pointing at Mom from across the kitchen table.

"I don't know . . . I just . . . spent it."

"On what? It was ten grand!"

"I don't . . ."

"You got something going on outside the house? Is that it? Are you dumping money on a girlfriend, you motherfucker?"

"You know that's not what it is! I would never . . ."
"Wouldn't you, Jeff?" Mom asked. "Wouldn't you?"

I've always hated the cliché of a man withering under his lover's gaze, but that's what happened. She didn't glare, but she also didn't blink. The old man died a little, right there on the yellowing linoleum floor, without anyone knowing until later.

"I wouldn't," he said again. "You know that."

"I don't know anything right now."

My mother is five-foot-six on your average day. She compressed a bit in that moment under some heavy fatigue of years of life spent thusly. She turned and walked out of the kitchen into the bedroom and shut the door. The mirror on that door is a triptych—three glass panels, each with part of a picture of a beat-up canoe floating in lake of green water. I've never noticed if that boat has oars.

Dad left quietly, without looking at me or bothering to plead his case at Mom's keyhole. Why didn't I ask where he was going? What would he have told me if I had? Instead I let him go. An hour later, I was showering to go out when Mom ran into the bathroom bawling into the phone. Dad was at his Post Office buddy Harry's house, gun in hand, talking about the end.

"Andrew tell him to come home! He needs to hear it from you—he won't listen to me!"

I didn't have the time to turn off the water or get out of the tub.

"Jesus, Dad, what is this? Give Harry the gun and come home."

I heard the click of Pop's holster unbuttoning and the drag of the pistol coming out. He'd been carrying it around the house; he must've or I'd have seen him go get it. *Wouldn't I?*

"Okay," he said. "He's got it."

"Leave it there and come home."

"Can you live with me if I do?"

"Yes."

"Do you love me?"

"Yes."

"Put your mother back on."

He proceeded to beg both forgiveness and permission. Forgiveness for the still-unexplained disappearance of all that money; permission to keep his gun. Eventually, after wearing her down, Mom relented.

"But I get to keep it and only I'll know where it is," she said.

He must've agreed because he walked into the house as I was leaving.

"Andrew," he said.

"Give her the goddamn gun and don't ever pull this again."

I kept walking.

I should've hugged my father then, shouldn't I? Gotten over my young rage, my bravado? Loved him, like I had said I did?

Instead, I got drunk. By the time I stumbled back home, I expected my parents to be asleep. What good are expectations if they aren't disappointed? When I walked in, Mom was marching on her treadmill watching Jerry Springer and Dad was taking a break from playing *Age of Empires* on the basement computer to make chocolate milk.

I was in dire need of a piss, but to get to the bathroom I'd have to cross paths with the kitchen. I glanced up at mom, sweating through her pink pajama shorts and Dad's Army PT shirt. She locked eyes with me, then gave a gentle nod toward where Dad was stirring his milk. "Go," she mouthed. She would allow me to pass it off as my idea, but I was called upon to make peace. I shuffled a few steps into the hall. *To pee before, or after?* I walked into the kitchen and went straight for the old man's chest with my forehead. Startled, he barely set down his thirty-ounce tumbler before I had him, as much as I could manage, in a bear hug.

"I don't want to have this conversation again, okay?" I said. I could hear the echo of my voice against his big body. His arms, much longer and meatier than mine, gave a squeeze around me. He could've expelled all the air from my lungs in that position. Made sure I'd never utter another word against him.

"Okay," he said instead.

"I have to take a leak, think you could let me go?"

The old man laughed and I did too.

"We okay?"

"Unless you want a night's worth of Pabst on your sock, you're gonna let go. We're fine, but I'm floating."

"Drain it, man," he said. "Don't forget to shake."

*

Inasmuch as one can forget a thing like that, we did. All of us, the whole incident. Until Pop began to itch like a dope fiend in withdrawal about the whereabouts of his revolver.

First he'd ask me. I honestly didn't know. Then he'd try to cajole me he'd make it seem like I was betraying the Old Boys Club of our family by letting Mom keep a secret. He ended up terrifying Mom into producing the weapon from the wicker laundry hamper at the foot of her bed.

"Jesus, Jeffrey, is it that important? We're not going to have another episode, are we?"

Episode. Great word for it, maybe the best. It really was like watching a movie—a perpetually blundering protagonist, at odds with his environs, loses his only source of comfort and has to embark on an epic quest to recover it. For Pop, it felt as such.

"No, I just . . . like to know where it is, just in case."

"You talk about shooting yourself again and I'll do it for you," I said.

How could I not have seen him for what he was? In that moment, he was afraid of me. He could've kicked my ass up and down the block, but I was enraged and he was taken far enough aback that I was the Drill Sergeant and he the lowly private. I was in charge under the dimshit fluorescent lights. How could I have missed it? It's hard to see what's cowering in front of you when it hides in such a big body. Hindsight.

Besides, that kind of shit only happens in movies. Right?

I murdered my father and I've only figured it out in this sentence.

"Don't talk about it, I told him. And he didn't.

I must fire my rifle TRUE.

It's a metacognitive pain in the ass to wonder why I wonder about the things I wonder about, why my revisitation of old traumas is so frequent, and why those backward voyages lead to forward-moving curiosities. I once considered myself capable of convincing myself of an answer to an unanswerable question; I could live in peace with whatever solution I sold myself, leave well-enough alone. But on the night that autumn really felt like itself that year, I found myself in the grass where my patio used to be—the paving stone patchwork Mom and I had laid and leveled ourselves when my grandmother was still alive; the meticulously-weeded rectangle in the shade of a dogwood tree; the ground on which my old man lay crumpled and dead on That Day—and I thought about how long it takes to die.

For some of us it's a finger snap, like my mom's cousin Buzz. Heart attack while shaking hands at a luncheon (for a few seconds I let myself wonder if anybody has luncheons anymore; I think not). He went out like Crazy Earl in *Full Metal Jacket*: sudden and without a lot of pain. Earl went down inspecting a stuffed bunny in the rubble gathered in a gangway between blown-out buildings. There was a boobytrap, because why wouldn't there be? Buzzy and Crazy Earl both gave up the ghost in the process of a perfunctory gesture. Buzz didn't care about the social grace of glad-handing, and Craze was only distracted by the out-of-placeness of the exploding rabbit. There was no intent, only execution.

For others, it's a drawn-out affair, like my father's mother who raged against death until a lethal kindness of morphine teetered her off the edge. It was seven hours after she was admitted to St. Mary's hospital for the last time. But it was months in the making: a near miss with double pneumonia after her husband died around Christmas, a move to my father's sister's compound in the quasi-rural suburbs up the hill from a trailer park, a few hundred needle sticks of dialysis, and the weight of everyone waiting for the inevitable.

I wondered about lethal injection for a while, and about how I'll vote if they try to repeal the death penalty in Missouri. I think about cyanide and strangulation, slitting wrists and drinking antifreeze margaritas. *How long does each of those take? Does it hurt to drown?*

It is this place that gets me thinking in this direction. It is the place, for sure, which winds everything back to the question I thought I had settled: *did my father suffer?* According to the Internet, there's no way to know. One blog says unless a self-inflicted gunshot is from a bazooka, there's bound to be agony. Another says even a .22 can make scrambled eggs out of the human brain quickly. Then there are quibbles over if it should be done gun to the temple or gun in the mouth. Gun in the mouth, for Pop. Aim for the throat versus aim for the cap of the skull. How could I know? Pop used to explain how it should be done, although he never intimated he'd learned for his own undoing.

"Mouth around the barrel, aim a couple inches above where your collar hits your neck."

That's what he said. Hints of help in the dead man's field manual, then.

*

June 15, 2017. I have made it fifteen years—a remarkable achievement. There should be a medal or a citation for this kind of thing. A graduation from survival school. But that would be too military. Too much bunting would be hung from the gutters of my house. I loathe bunting. And by now I'm too old to fancy that "Over It" is a place I can ever reach. I am only, at times, concerned with not becoming my father. Not unbecoming alive by choice. But the fight is real, the temptation to cross over always there. I don't feel it tonight, but I don't feel much in the way of a vital impulse.

It is dark and the wind is cool. Morning is not far off, but in no hurry to be here, either. In Battle Creek, my friend Steph is mid-shift at Bronson Hospital. She will answer her phone for me; I know this.

It rings and I imagine her scrub bottom pocket flashing and shaking, the skin on her thigh tingle-tensing and her control of her face muting everything in front of her patient. I also imagine her in a supply closet, texting her daughter and being modestly delighted I called.

It rings and I imagine the quietude of having to answer everything—forever—myself.

Before the third ring ends, Steph picks up, an intrusion on invention that will lead to revelation.

"Hi, hold on," she says. I can hear her work phone chirping in the background. Steph gives another nurse some numbers and measures. "Hey, sorry, I've got a lady downstairs who's probably going to code soon. What's up?"

"I need help," I say.

"If it's bail money, I'm in Michigan. And if you're locked up here, you'll be dead by the time I get there anyway."

I like listening to her laugh. It's genuine, a study in what it sounds like to be joyful. Truncating a moment like this is not easy for me, but neither was making the call.

"I need you to tell me what happens when someone shoots themselves."

I'm sure she's about to invoke jargon outside my purview and start referencing neurotransmitters or various cortexes, lobes, and nerve clusters, finding a sterile way to explain grim death.

"Generally it kills them. As you know."

"Does it hurt, Steph? Did my dad . . ."

"Okay, whoa. I can answer this, but you've got to be sure you want me to. What brought this up?"

"I don't know, but it's here now."

Steph is only quiet for a second. She is unafraid, even of the truth. Too many nights staring into it through sucking chest wounds and tracheotomy tubes. She is about to give me facts, nothing more.

"Temple or mouth?"

"Mouth."

"Good. Open casket?"

"Yup." I nod without trying to.

"What kind of weapon?"

"Six inch .38."

"Ah, damn. That's a small gun. That's not necessarily good news. Did you read the autopsy report?"

"No. God no. Why would I do that?"

"To answer questions like this I would need to know, as exactly as I could, where the exit wound was. There's only a slim chance he could've found the Sweet Spot."

"You mean the medulla?"

"Mmhm. Medical base of the brain."

"I think he knew where to aim."

"Well, he's not one of the amateurs that comes through my doors, then. He must've done some research and had some pretty steady nerves. But, if he was trying to put it through the bullseye, there's a decent chance he did. In which event, probably no pain. After trigger pull, you're looking at six or seven minutes of nerve information that can come in. Touch and sound go last."

"He could've heard birds?"

"Sure. And felt breeze, or the ground under him. Outside stimuli, not pain. By the way, what direction was he facing?"

"God, I don't know. He tried to teach me cardinal directions and it didn't go well. That's how I ended up doing

Driver's Ed through Sears. 'East, boy, East' got nobody anyplace."

"I mean what was he looking at? What would've been in front of him?"

"Oh. The house. Our back porch is a decent size and enclosed. We'd actually just had a new roof put on it. There's a dormer on the back side of the house that goes from the attic onto said roof, and I always wanted to crawl out there and smoke a cigarette but the attic is creepy as fuck. White with blue trim. That's the color of the house. My mom's bedroom window is at a forty-five to the spot where Dad . . ."

"Did she hear it?"

"No. Nobody did, not even our neighbors. Todd—he doesn't live there anymore on account of the skinny Leukemia survivor he was married to divorcing him—was a construction worker and would've been leaving for work around then. Or maybe he was gone already. I don't know, dude."

"Where were you?"

"Sleeping in what's now my office. I couldn't stand it being my bedroom afterward. Too much guilt for not waking up until . . . after."

"Okay, okay. Sorry. Let's get back on the rails. If my experience is worth anything, I could venture to say that your dad saw your house last. It was the image he wanted to die with and he got it."

"You're telling me the truth, right?"

"Only always."

"Thanks. I think I'll lie here awhile longer. And Steph? Do you think he looked in on me before he went outside?"

"Yes."

"How do you know?"

"I don't. You didn't ask me to prove it, you asked what I thought. Anybody who planned to the minutest detail would've looked."

"What if he didn't?"

"You're wallowing."

"Not anymore. I'm not obsessing, either."

"Nice. Well, listen, I'll call you tomorrow. I've got to change some catheters and eat my lunch."

"Why do you tell me all the stuff I didn't ask?"

"My fee for services rendered. Long distance office visits mean you have to hear about bodily fluids and deli meat."

"I love you."

"Goodnight."

*

What happens after the dial tone is no miracle. I stay in the yard, watching the night and listening to the streetlights hum. *If this is the last sensation I feel, will I die happy?* I try to replicate Dad's last body position down to the adjustment for where his gut was bigger than mine.

Here. Now. This can be a permanence. Would I be relieved? Would I?

Steph calls back.

"Are you alright? I just figured out what day it is."

"I'm cool. Just in my head."

"Keep everything in there that's supposed to be."

"I'm cool, seriously."

"Promise."

I like how she doesn't ask but tells.

"I promise."

I must SHOOT STRAIGHTER . . .

I didn't want to go. It was early, it was Saturday, I was off work all day. But it was the old man's birthday gift: a trip to the range with his favorite revolver and his favorite child.

"You look like you got after it last night," the old man said as I wandered into the living room. "Sure you're up for this?"

"I'm fine. Could use a silencer for everything, but I'll manage. We should eat and get coffee first."

"You buying? I'm a little flat until payday."

"Yeah, that's cool, I'll spring for you."

"We might have to go Dutch on targets and shells, too."

I nodded and felt my brain beat against my skull. Between allergies and a hangover I was in a bad way.

"Roger that, just let me hose off real quick."

When I'd showered, dry heaved, and dressed, Pop had both of our pistols in their carry cases and was wearing his Missouri Army National Guard cap.

"Lock and load," he said.

"Did you shine your boots for this, too?"

"I'll shine them with your ass when we get there."

*

Off the highway by less than a mile was the Blue Owl Café. Calling it quaint would be a sin against folksy establishments in similar corners of middle America. But the coffee was strong, the biscuits and gravy came pronto, and with a tip for Gracie, the ninety-six-year-old waitress, everything cost me twenty bucks. While we ate, Dad goaded me. I was not going shooting with my father, I was going to duel with him.

"I always told you there'd be a day where you'd take me out in the alley and test your nuts," he said.

Today was that day, whether I knew it, liked it, wanted it, or not.

*

I misremember everything except how this episode came to a close. Much of it is reconstructed from dust and bad lighting.

The range was called Top Gun; it was ritzy, as these places go. Had a lot of rentable firearms, most of which were big, phallic, assault type weapons. They had a special going that day where one could rent a Desert Eagle .50 handgun and get free targets. I don't remember how much that cost.

Pop and I got adjacent stalls and, for the first few magazines, we were alone in our spaces. But I could feel the glances coming through the divider, the old man's eyes stretching downrange to assess my accuracy. My father was Hartman leaning on Gomer Pyle's shoulder. Soon he laid his weapon down and came up behind me.

"It's time," he said.

There was a ritual involved that I could feel but not describe—a reverence in the way Pop hung the targets and sent them to their various distances from the firing line. After each round of firing he'd bring the paper enemies back on their remote-controlled ziplines and count our point totals.

"You kill me in the longshots," I said.

"Longer barrel helps. And I think between pulls. You're rushing like you have to be someplace."

"Nah. I figure if I'm confident enough to pull the trigger once, I'm not going to move that much between shots. Empty the clip and either you were right or you weren't."

Pop loaded his pistol without looking at the cylinder.

"Makes sense," he said. "Alright, last one. Combat distance."

By this he meant seven yards. According to Pop, most gunfights occur within twenty-one feet. We were tied on points going into the final. But I destroyed the old man when it counted. Eight bullseyes, six nines, and an eight. Pop came up short by two points when it was over.

"Think you missed one altogether," I said. "Pulled it or something."

"I had you," he said. "Fucking had you all the way."

"I just got lucky I aimed right the first time. Trusted my hands."

"Close counts, alright. I had you."

"Same time next week?"

"Go ahead. Brag. Get it out."

"Hey I didn't want to come in the first place, man, let alone get into a pissing contest. You're mad you piddled on the seat. Sucks for you."

Dad put his hand out and I left it hang there in gunpowder and echoes for a second before shaking it.

"Nicely done, son," he said.

"I'm sorry."

"Can it. You were the better man today. Congratulations."

Somewhere, Gunnery Sergeant Hartman was crowing: my gunny had finally found my sinister talent.

. . . than MY ENEMY . . .

To plead guilty or not? Is that self-aggrandizing? Pop had many enemies. It's not really fair to assume I was the one he feared most. I have to acknowledge the invisible *They* Pop warned me about as a child.

"Never go home the same way three days in a row. That's how *They* get your routine. And then one day you come home and *They* are waiting for you on the porch and it's too late to turn back."

Like Kubrick's Marines, Dad got a peculiar stare when he gave these sermons, as if seeing past what was there and into some terrifying otherness.

"Who are *They?*" I'd ask.

"Let's hope you never find out."

*

"He was always doing that type of shit," Tim says. "He used to hide screwdrivers and ten-penny nails behind dumpsters in the alleys we'd cut through to get to school. I mean, like, elementary school."

Tim is my second-youngest uncle and he's drinking my whiskey in my kitchen.

"Who was he scared of?"

"Everybody."

*

It's fair to say love is conditional most of the time. Love was my old man's nemeses—it's fluttering, fleeting, fickleness. The violence that could replace it. Dad's own father was his enemy. He wielded a belt, a short temper, and a resentment of his second-oldest son that became a misplaced rage and a stinging memory.

Pop played football for his father. Joined the Air Force for his father. Took beatings which belonged to my oldest uncle Dave. When these didn't win a consistent heart from my grandfather, Dad became a father himself to prove he could un-be the thing that raised him.

My father's mother was the enemy too. Her weapons were silence, cigarettes, and needlework. Mostly silence. Norma was a phone, off the hook. An apology unoffered. She was the wounding type of guiltless.

It's no shock that Dad's siblings were enemies, both Dad's and one another's. But how much of that was self-inflicted? Pop was his own enemy too. Afraid to forgive, afraid to love, afraid to be wrong. The Smarts were given unto one another a sameness, and that sameness sent them to one another's throat.

*

My father's perception of a decent man was one who put food on the table, clothes on our backs, didn't drink, cheat, or beat my mother or myself. But being a decent man was also tied to belongings. Emotional availability wasn't part of the bargain:

ready money was. That was weaponized against the old man at some point—began to backfire. It was the tank sent to quell the rebellion of unreality. We were not rich in dollars and we were increasingly poor in our bonds. Failure was sent to knock and my father was terrified of answering the door.

. . . who is trying to **KILL ME.**

It's not of the body all the time, but of the aura or the self-image. Vestigial assassinations that accrue over our endless numbered days. One against an army was my father's fight.

I MUST SHOOT HIM, BEFORE HE SHOOTS ME.

What a clusterfuck of pronouns. There are too many "him's" and "me's" on the table to accurately assign an identity to any of them. "He" could mean me (look, it's a mess already), the adultish son who threatens the father's dominance. Or it could be Dad's ideal self, the indefatigable strongman who can outwit everything and everyone, and if that's the way we draw it up, "me" is my actual-factual father—the body, the bluster, the decay of the façade, impending admission of failures old and new. That's a redundant discrepancy; it's as oxymoronic as overcoming self-preservation in an attempt to save your legacy or telling your son in a note to finish building the second bathroom with your life insurance so you'll be remembered every time someone in the basement takes a dump. It's as nonsense as war or crying for the ghosts of our loved ones. It's perfectly sane and that's the problem.

I WILL.

If the shortest verse in the Bible is "Jesus wept," then the shortest verse of my father's apocrypha is "I will."

I should've known how he'd go out, man. Everyone should've. Look at the samurai movies, for one. Seppuku, Hari Kiri—the old man loved that shit. Or Civil War flicks; confederate foot soldiers marching into cannons and Old Glory to defend their molasses accents and their honor. Pop was wicked into that. And Gomer Pyle exploding his head onto the wall of a Marine Corps shithouse? Mesmerizing to Dad.

"If the food ever doesn't taste good or I can't wipe my ass, give me whiskey and my pistol. I'm not waiting around after that," he'd say.

I never saw him eating less in those last months, but I saw less of him at all. He was big enough that if he'd lost twenty pounds, who would know? And it was inconceivable that he'd been depressed enough to miss meals. Let alone follow through on a fatalistic mission statement.

He was full of that bravado, the machismo of a guy who was secretly ashamed of himself. Freud called it "reaction formation"—the louder you whistle in the dark, the more afraid of it you are.

When the old man pulled the trigger, he called everybody's bluff.

"I'll teach you about what it takes to hack it," I'm sure he thought about thinking.

"I will."

He did.

I weep.

Before GOD . . .

God is more concept than concrete in the house of my childhood. Not for me, of course. I am drilled on my catechism and my New International Translation of the Bible. I am baptized, I am confirmed into the Lutheran Church of the Missouri Synod, I am an acolyte, a crucifer, a sexton, and (until dropping out in 2001) a pre-seminary student. My father has the dogma of the military; I have theology.

*

The old man was raised in a Methodist church by agnostic parents, but he behaved like a Baptist, didn't trust Catholics, thought Pentecostals were obnoxious, and settled on Lutheranism because my mother told him to and there was nothing he really hated about it. He dug the rituals: shirt and tie Sunday, saying grace before meals, candlelit vigils on Good

Friday. But for him, God was a backburner presence. God was only there to pass judgment on those who were morally defective.

On Christmas Day, Hartman gives his recruits a history lesson: God predates the Marines, but the Marines still own the recruits. Love the Lord, but serve the Corps.

Priorities.

Kubrick's, not my father's.

The film's, not my director's.

Someone's, not mine.

Someone needs to get right with the idea of God.

*

God comes back to Leona Street in the form of Pastor Tim. He is here to administer the sacrament of communion and welcome us to our new church after we flee our old one.

"Lot of many memories, most of them funerals. Everybody's disappointment when I left Sem prep. I need something new," I say.

"I can't go back there. Ever," Mom says.

"I understand. At Epiphany we . . ."

"Do you think my husband went to Hell?"

God is now the elephant in the room. Pastor is still. His beard is down to his clerical, making me wonder what he did before the cloth.

"No," he says. "I do not."

"Thank God," Mom says.

"What makes you think so?" I ask. "Luther tells us . . ."

"What does Luther tell us?"

God is my foot in my mouth.

"Well, in the Apology to the Augsburg Confession, I thought there was something . . ."

"I wrote my doctoral dissertation on biblical suicide and I haven't been defrocked; I must be on to something, yeah?"

"I'd like to read it."

"It's probably in the Seminary library, if you really want. The important part isn't the scholarship, it's the comfort I want you to take away from this. Insofar as you still believe in God or Heaven, I believe your father is there."

Mom takes my hand. God is her palm against my own.

"Thank you," she says.

Pastor doesn't hear her or isn't ready to.

"Do you?" he asks me.

"Do I what?"

"Still have your faith?"

"Yes. It's a different faith, by necessity. But it's there."

"We should have a beer some time. Talk about the malleability of believing."

. . . I swear THIS CREED

Creed: noun; a set of basic principles or beliefs; a guiding mantra.

Each night I'd pretend to sleep and my old man would pretend to buy it. He'd tuck me in, mummifying me into a helpless tickling target. I'd snore; it was one of those chainsaw-meets-a-fart-sound snores that wasn't believable for a second. And Dad would tickle me into a tizzy until I'd thrashed myself out of my straitjacket and into a position to sleep. He'd kiss my forehead and make the sign of the cross.

"God and Daddy will watch over you tonight," he'd say.

It was not the only time his voice could be close to a coo, but the earliest times I remember—and the fondest—are these.

I was raised to believe in an afterlife. From some elevated vantage God and Daddy still have my back. But the tangibles are missed, although they died off before my father did. The affections. The expressions. Closing my eyes to footsteps moving only a thin wall away, then standing guard. This is romance. Bullshit. I know. How many times did Dad fall asleep on the job? How many times did he promise a thing he could not deliver? What reasons did I have to feel safe in my sleep after he crept away in the just-dawn and abandoned me?

I have no answer except that I cannot unlearn all the sureness of faith. Sometimes I try to abandon it, give in to myself and the all-too-obvious fact that most of this life makes no sense. I know I could not be a preacher anymore. I can only pray myself into enough of a calm to tide me over from one moment to the next.

But I really want to know; when I pray to my father who art in heaven, which one am I calling for?

MY RIFLE AND MYSELF . . .

I wish Kubrick would've used the full version of the Rifleman's creed—selfishly because it's richer and I could use the sinews and muscle to bury and resurrect my father deeper and more completely in and with the film, but also because there is much more there to reinforce this theme of union between shooter and firearm. But this snippet was enough, alongside the rest of the film and a gun-toting American ethos, to seduce Pop into a sordid identity crisis.

. . . are the DEFENDERS . . .

Defenders. That's rich.

Was Holden Caulfield's hat some kind of superhero cape? Of course not, it was a symbol. Does Linus become invisible when he hides under his threadbare blue blanket? Fuck no. Same with my old man's gun: an object imbued with no particular value except what he gave it. It was an aggressor, with its phallus of a barrel. It was a penis pump, a hard-on pill. I might as well have loaded maximum strength Viagra into the chambers and shot the old man in the dick with them. Defender, hell.

Pop was no great shield against disaster. When my maternal grandma died, he crumbled worse than Mom or me. He used Maw's death as an excuse for pissing away hundreds of bucks on network marketing scams.

"I had to figure out how to replace her social security checks," he said. Who was protecting whom? A federal employee in his prime hiding behind an old lady's pittance.

Even in death he couldn't live up to the hype. Every USPS employee of Dad's generation had the option to choose a life insurance policy of up to five times their maximum salary while in the employ of the Postal Service; when dad shot himself, Mom and I found out our fearless provider had only opted for a policy worth three times the max. It's callous to talk dollars over a dead body, but it was a thing Pop would forecast. He would allude to the comforts he'd afford us by dying someday, the great dump the postal eagle would take in our checking account.

*

Now I need to check myself. I'm angry. I feel like maybe I just became Joker in the opening scene of *Full Metal Jacket*. I tried to let you see my war face, just now, but it didn't work, did it? Nah. I remember reading somewhere that Philip Gerard had to retool his essay "What They Don't Tell You About Hurricanes" for over a year to weed out the raw rage. Nobody wants to read a writer who's all pissed-off, Gerard said. It's not art. I am not being fair to my dad. I am not good, kind, or capable enough for that.

Anger is a flame that only makes shadow puppets possible.

Until I can put that anger out, I will fold my hands and make a bushel. Maybe the light can hide just this once. This little light of mine. I'm going to let it shine. Just not tonight.

. . . of MY COUNTRY.

America, right? Or is this another entry in my father's postmortem dictionary of multi-entendres?

Country: noun, a territory to which one pledges allegiance or from whence one is descended; also: noun, a place toward which one feels a pull of patriotic duty, which compels one to act in ways otherwise out of character.

It's America, yes. Dad loved it, even in its fucked-upness. But it's smaller than that. It's our house, my father's kingdom. Deadbolts and bullets would protect it. But I think my father's country was his person if I'm using all my senses. He was the autonomous, self-possessed, Isle of Jeffrey. Dad's country was water, blood, belly fat, brain matter, and a little plastic sign reading "No Trespassing."

His autopsy was the rape of a motherland too stingy to give the marauding coroner anything to keep.

Country: noun, a place defined by its people. When one is the other, there is a dearth of both.

WE ARE THE MASTERS of our enemy.

It was always about this—dominance. Rulership. Pop had all the pithy *isms* to back him: "I don't have to be right, I'm your father," and such. But he was tethered to his notion of what that meant, controlled by conventions he feared and manipulated by features he did not have. Joining forces with the gun did not make him a co-pilot of his vessel, but a stowaway inside the body of a maniac captain. Gun was master, shooter was servant. When it became thus, I can't say. But that it did is obvious, at least right now.

We are the SAVIORS . . .

To denigrate a term with such exalted connotations is a dick move. What did my father and his pistol save?

They saved time, of course. They saved maybe decades of time—time spent aging and decaying, losing more each day. Dad died at fifty-two, way before incontinence or cancer, open-heart surgery or insulin pumps, walkers, or hearing aids. He could pretend to be of sound body while he was quietly losing his mind and his family.

Did they save Dad's legacy, too? With my mother, I think they did. She misses him with muscles of emotion I did not know a human could possess. She sighs for him, refuses to date, insists she is a married woman. If the old man had lived these last ten years, Mom would've almost certainly walked out on him, but his deadness makes her unremember the emotional abuses, the fiscal stupidities, the thoughtlessness, and the skid marks in Dad's underpants.

"He was an asshole," Mom admits. "But he was my asshole."

She is no emotional simpleton, my mother. But she's also not as good at grudge holding as her son is. For me, feeling my fingertip against the steel of a trigger is now almost repugnant, and I blame my father. I resent him every time my mother cries for him, every time a donation envelope from the Democratic Party of Missouri comes in his name.

I have learned to love my father always, while hating him often. From this there is no salvation. For Dad or for me.

. . . of MY LIFE.

Let's replace this with life*style*. You couldn't go on without an honesty you were never prepared for, so you fell on your sword. You never cared for your physical existence; that wasn't life to you. Life was dying when you chose, after doing as you pleased. Smith, Wesson, and you might've saved your life after all, in the world according to you, which really was the only one that mattered.

SO BE IT.

Que sera sera.

Let it be.

It's out of my hands.

It is what it is.

*

Triteness without end in the face of one man's resolve and his surviving family's new normal. Pop used to school me in military acronyms when I was a boy. One of his favorites, and mine, was FIDO: Fuck It, Drive On. Toward the end of the Parris Island segment of *Full Metal Jacket*, Hartman is berating Pyle into finishing a run.

He keeps screaming and Pyle keeps stumble-running.

One foot in front of the other.

Left, right, left, right, left.

Fuck it. Drive on.

Until there is NO ENEMY . . .

Come back and tell me who this was, old man.

When I visit your grave, I only hear the wind and some noise from the freeway, maybe a barge on the Mississippi pulling at her mooring chains. I leave Oreos and pennies on your headstone. Once I left a tall can of Pabst. I thought you'd have spoken to me in your fake southern drawl by now, but you haven't, and I wonder if it's because you think I never listened when you tried to talk in life.

I listened, Pop. I just thought you were wrong. Still do.

. . . but PEACE.

Peace is the old cliché of church pews and graveyards. Peace be with you (*And also with you*). Rest in Peace. I hate the number of 'peaces' there are. The individuation of pastorals and tranquilities from person to person, era to era. From life to life and death to death. Why couldn't peace be a rocking chair and baseball on the radio? Why couldn't it have been barbecues and saying grace while holding hands? For my father, peace was the absence of war and there was war all the time, everywhere.

Victory and defeat had to conflate into one reagent: my father's peace.

*

In *FMJ*, the marines move along the Perfume River in a Kubrickian irony. In South St. Louis, I drive drunk along a drainage ditch called River des Peres. It is not French for 'Despair'; it is Half Orphan Speak for "Shit Creek."

AMEN.

My catechism tells me this means "Yes, yes, it shall be so."

We say it to affirm that we have faith that the prayer we have just breathed or brained is what God would have willed us to pray. The marines in *Full Metal Jacket* gave the Amen to Hartman. My father gave it to the gun. I hold it in my mouth, paining my chest. I cannot give permission to the Already.

*

I expect a column of tanks to pass by my house, a platoon of grunts behind it with M-14s and Marlboro's banded to their helmets. I expect cinematography and a score. A director's chair and one of those fancy, flying-cameraman rigs.

I get azaleas, dog shit, and the neighborhood watch. It's either dawn or sundown. It's either about to be yesterday or just finishing up tomorrow. I am Private Joker, humping out of the film:

The world has gone to shit, but I'm alive. Yes. Ame

LULLABY FOR THE MASSES

Full Metal Jacket begins with a twang. Johnny Wright's crooning, folky voice glazes over a montage of new Marine recruits being relieved of their coifs by a largely invisible military barber. Their faces blank, their locks falling to the floor with prescribed lyricism, it is easy to watch the young men and block out the music. But from the outset, Kubrick's tragicomic war film is rife with sneaky, not-quite-subliminal suggestiveness.

The lyrics to Wright's tune "Hello Vietnam" are more than just a little saccharine for the strychnine to come; they are a resignation to the impermanence of joy, a disparate mixture of jingoism and jadedness. "America has heard the bugle call," Wright intones. It's' an innocuous thing—conjuring up images of Radar O'Reilly mangling reveille on M*A*S*H, or a lone horn blower honoring a dead soldier with Taps. It's gentle, out of context.

The co-hook doesn't frighten either: "Kiss me goodbye and write me when I'm gone." It's an homage to every war movie cliché: troops in the field swooning over pictures of their gals, folding and refolding love letters in a wartime origami that can only exist *in situ*. A nod to the frail hope that love conquers all and to the tradition of filmmakers' dashing of said hopes by killing off at least one (usually more) of the lovesick GIs.

But the song veers, if only for a few bars, into pragmatism:

"I don't believe that war will ever end. There's fighting that will break us up again."

Johnny Wright, sly devil. Stanley Kubrick, movie house mastermind.

After forty-five seconds of lulling the audience into a sense of only mild discomfort, the singer and the director conspire to introduce what will be an echoed motif: the enduring existence of war and those who fight it; the gung-ho bloodlust of some who command armies; precarious balances between safety and harm; mortality hastened by conflict; expendability rationalized by the ethos of duty. It's a small thing on paper. A thimbleful of words slipped into the song's—and, ergo, the film's—toddlerhood. But it's huge because of the shadow it begins to cast.

I'm looking for what I believe and finding it as a consequence. Maybe not. Janet Maslin, longtime *New York Times* movie critic and giant in her field, made note of the song's inclusion in *Full Metal Jacket* in her 1987 review of the film. "Corny," she called it, and "lulling." But Maslin quickly moved from the impact of the track and into her vastly insightful commentary on the camera angles and the "sleeping white light" that pervades not only the first scene, but the entire opening act.

It's the haste with which we dispatch the musical accompaniment to the film's beginning that bothers me most. The bugle call: Vietnam America heard it but also questioned the timing, the caller, and the cause. "A hill to be taken, a battle to be won." That's a sinister allusion to the innumerable firebases and landing zones American troops would fight and die to clear or defend. Read Karl Marlantes' *Matterhorn* or Tim O'Brien's *The Things They Carried* for brilliant, literary, and timely examples. Watch the 2011 documentary *Restrepo* for a present-day instance.

Beside the allusions and the foreshadowing, Wright's song is a prototypically Kubrickian double-entendre. Many lyrics are drenched in irony and satire—if you want them to be. Take, for instance, "I hope and pray someday the world will learn / That fires we don't put out will bigger burn / We must save freedom now at any cost / Or someday our own freedom will be lost." For the generations born or living in post-Vietnam America, this logic is so threadbare it's laughable. But, for the marines depicted in *Full Metal Jacket*, it was quite possibly a credo worth dying for.

Throughout the film, Kubrick continues the war-within-a-war between rhetoric and realism. To do this though, the director needs this largely underappreciated musical preamble. Wright's primary hook, "Goodbye my sweetheart, hello Vietnam," is code for any number of brutalities:

"Goodbye children, hello hardened grunts.

Goodbye breathing, hello cheap pine box.

Goodbye reason, hello just move and react."

And, for my father, my mother, and myself: Goodbye "it's just a movie," hello *FMJ*.

Platoon 3092 and others will again bear themselves across the screen to a seemingly mismatched theme song in the film's denouement; as Ellison writes, "the end is in the beginning, and lies far ahead."

Goodbye, my sweetheart. Hello, Vietnam.

*

I didn't realize until someone else told me (isn't that the story of my life?) that it isn't just the opening track that drives the ironic layering and suggestiveness of *Full Metal Jacket*. My partner Lisa called me shortly after watching the movie for the first time.

"Holy shit," she said. "I mean, really. Holy shit. He used every song my dad plays on repeat at the farm. It's the soundtrack of that whole generation."

"There's only like two songs in the whole movie though. There's Johnny Wright at the beginning, a few lines from the Mickey Mouse club theme at the end, and "Paint it Black" by the Rolling Stones over the end credits."

"Honey, I love you, but you're busy knowing it all that; you're not learning very much."

"You're nothing if not honest."

"Look at it: 'These Boots Are Made for Walking,' 'Wooly Bully,' 'Surfin' Bird,' 'Chapel of Love.'" There's a ton going in there. It's all the songs they'd have been playing at sock-hops or high school mixers, but the soldiers in the movie didn't get to go to those. Your dad did, though. I wonder if hearing those songs but seeing that movie was like a trigger or something. Some kind of extra guilt that he didn't fight."

The light shone.

While I do not have the right to say Stanley Kubrick produced this genius irony on purpose, I can point to it in awe. Kubrick creates a dichotomy between the radios that play music and the radios humped through the jungle by marines in combat. The first belts out catchy—if often subtly apropos to the themes of the film, especially in the case of the Nancy Sinatra number—tunes; the latter is a vehicle for disenchantment.

I look to the scene in the ruins of Hue City, shortly before the Viet Cong sniper appears. Cowboy, who's taken over control of the Lusthog Squad, calls in to command for tank support.

He says something like *gimme the goddamn radio* and swears at the Marine on the other end of the transmission as he details their situation. But there is no tank. No help. There's only a crackling voice of another marine who is seated somewhere else, like a sinister disc jockey who refuses to play the only song that will save the day.

Cowboy is left with only one word (which allegedly only appears in the film about ninety times although I think it's much higher):

"Fuck."

And as the film crew within the film documents the action of combat, "Surfin' Bird" by The Trashmen plays. I notice the staccato, plosive "B" sounds that almost replicate machine gun fire, but don't quite. Also, the multitudinous meanings for "bird": the middle finger, air support, medivac choppers, a colonel, the plane that takes discharged marines back stateside—The Sweet Bird of Freedom. All tucked inside pop culture and laid over the horror of its alternative.

I could go on delving into how each song works in the context of the film, but I won't. The truth is, I wouldn't have done that before Lisa pointed out that it was at least worth noticing. It'd be disingenuous to start earning my PhD in film studies now. But I'll admit to having read a book about the myriad ways Kubrick incorporates music and sound effects into his films. I'll cop to hearing Johnny Wright in my head every time I get my hair cut.

*

Phillip Lopate speaks of film as "an extension of American letters." In my study of literature, it's always been stressed that the ethos surrounding a piece is almost as important as the piece itself. Therefore, given the saturation, subversion, and overlap of the ethos of the '60s and the ethos of the '80s (and beyond, out to posterity), Stanley Kubrick's *Full Metal Jacket* maintains the tradition of connectivity between film and the page. If I were pressed to say, what movies do, I'd align myself with Lopate and Kubrick:

Movies carry the weight of literature and cultural testimony or criticism. They fuck with you, tease you, echo your life or the lives you wish you'd lived. Movies—ones aimed more at art than blockbusting—live because their subjects are the endless foibles and dilemmas of the human condition.

This is why, paradoxically and permanently, I remain like Lopate: a happy captive of the theater.

FULL MOTHER JACKET

The summer I turned ten, it dawned on me that if my father was any of the men in *Full Metal Jacket*, my mother was the crassest allusion to women: Mary Jane Rottencrotch. I didn't get the balls to say that out loud until years later, but it was an inside joke I shared with myself all the same. Mary Jane shows up first on Parris Island. As Hartman is tucking the recruits into bed with their rifles, he has an order like this to bellow:

Give your weapon a girl's name,[1] because she's the only woman in your life. Mary Jane Rottencrotch and her pink underpants are gone. You're wed to your weapon, until death do you part.

---

[1] Gomer Pyle's rifle is named Charlene. My mom is called Janet Rae. It almost pains me that Mom and the woman Gomer slept next to when he could close his eyes and forget she was a rifle never had a chance to meet. They never met and still, occasioned by the unfolding of the universe, their shadows are forever overlapped. They could've worn the same lipstick and braided one another's hair. Of course not.

Mary Jane.[2] She's the vanilla stand-in for every girl next door, high school sweetheart, and lover's lane hand job dispenser in America.[3] Rottencrotch, though? Since my first time watching the film, I've wondered why Kubrick would defile such an outwardly wholesome image.

The women we meet in *Full Metal Jacket* only number three. Two are snipers and the third is a hooker who cripples and slaughters Doc Jay and Eightball; despite the presences of

---

[2]Mary Jane in the script, Mama Jan in the world. Have I been calling my mother a sing-song cousin of her forbear all this time? I have. Have I constructed this parallel and let it be a load-bearing beam in the construct of my life? I have. I am my father's son, whether he would have me or not. Whether I would or wouldn't claim him. We are a we, and there is no killing, backspacing, film editing, or unremembering to change this.

[3]Mom was the high school sweetheart. Dad laid eyes on her in Mr. Mogelnicki's homeroom in 1969, then spent four years pining and pestering his way into what Mom swears were never her *pink panties*. "White. Always white. It's what my mother could afford and what my grandmother approved of. Hell, I still only wear white undies." "She played tonsil hockey on the first date," Dad once told me. I could've died without knowing. The two married in '73 after a year of courtship that began with my old man sending word to Cleveland High's studentry that anyone wishing to date Janet Andre would have to go through him. "I've never regretted your father. But I think Steve Fernandez was sweet on me and God he was good looking. He ended up in the FBI, did I ever tell you that?" Once or twice, Ma. Once or twice.

a triumvirate of females, *FMJ* is a male movie, for all that means.[4]

Hooker number one sashays across the frame as the second act of the film opens. Joker and Rafterman are at a café table and the young woman approaches them with the straight-from-central-casting line:

Hey baby.

She tosses the back of her short leather skirt in the air and poses for Rafterman's booty pics, blows kisses, really sells her bill of goods.

She promises fellatio, oral, head, dome, brain. She'll suck it and she won't quit on it. She'll love on the dusty Marines for as long as it takes. Love on them a long, long time. She doesn't need as many words as that to articulate her meaning, but as soon as she starts her pitch the synapses in the sex-starved brains of Joker and Rafterman produce vivid bonus verbiage.

So as not to seem purely businesslike, the hooker adds one more promise:

---

[4]I'm thinking specifically of the scene at Parris Island where Hartman leads the recruits around the barracks in their underwear; they're marching, holding their rifles, and honking their cocks. They sing an alternating rhyme about which instrument is for killing and which one is for sex Every time they get to the sex verse, they give their boxer-clad cocks a honk. And there's always the reveille ordering the troops to drop their cocks and pull up their socks, which Dad used on me before school in the mornings. I always thought it was funny that I only had one cock and two socks, but somehow he didn't see the discrepancy. Whatever.

She so horny!

Whether this cliché was born in Kubrick's film or not I cannot say, but it is the most famous appearance thereof; this is to say, the first woman the audience of *Full Metal Jacket* encounters is in no way unique. She is to be seen, appraised, toyed with, and forgotten. She is a device.

The second prostitute appears in the waning scenes of the movie, as a weary mix-and-match Lusthog squad of Joker, Cowboy, Animal Mother, Eightball, and others lounge outside a bombed-out movie theatre. Unlike her predecessor, the second girl is represented by a pimp—a soldier in the South Vietnamese Army.

Any you boys want A-number-one sexy, he asks Cowboy and the crew burst into a chorus of adlib hoots and hollers. Of course, a pack of field Marines want number one sexy. As Joker and Rafterman did with Hooker number one, the gang makes certain the sequel sex worker will give them the good time of their liking.

The ARVN pimp assures the boys his lady's vagina isn't prude or stingy: they can suck on it, fuck it, blow smoke rings up it. Anything they want, as long as they want. For fifteen dollars each. Again, as with the first business transaction, here begins the bartering. Cowboy, the spokes-John, counters that fifteen bucks is *beaucoup* money and lowballs the pimp in return: a group rate of five dollars per man. Naturally, the pimp comes back with ten, leaving Cowboy to decide whether to acquiesce and guarantee himself and his squad some *poontang* or keep the bargain alive.

Five dollars, Cowboy says. Or some rifles that've never been shot and only dropped one time, maybe two.

He leans back in his theatre seat. The pimp, defeated, accepts.

Until this point, the hooker herself is only a body. She's there, in the picture, but she's silent. Her attire is unremarkable: a yellowish tank top, purple capris, big sunglasses. She is attractive without being memorable; like the one before her, this young woman is not unique. She does, however, exhibit some personality—some tragic sense of depth—before the scene closes. Eightball, a large Black grunt, is all too eager to be her first customer. But the pimp translates his girl's Vietnamese, saying something like: No brothers allowed in the coochie. Too [5] Black men: boo coo, no can do.

As a kid watching this scene I was lost for how to feel. Should I be cock-shamed by the inference that Black men are hung better than me, or laugh because a small Asian man is telling a Black guy that his man parts are too big for an even smaller Asian woman? Should I feel any kind of way at all?

A couple decades later, I feel this: pain. It doesn't take a gynecologist to know there's only so much expansion a vagina is capable of; beyond that, it tears. In addition to getting gangbanged, this hooker had her crotch destroyed. I wish this made her special. How many girls with too much perfume

---

[5] Multiple spellings of *buku* (the most widely accepted vernacular) are in common use. I'm partial to *boo coo*; something about the elongation, the space between monosyllables. Especially when it's used to describe an oversized penis. Too big? Two words.

and too few options sold their body to the violence and its executors? The girls and their pimps call it "loving." She love you good, she love you long, she love you too much. But there is no love here.

Eventually Animal Mother takes the hooker by the arm and marches her toward the theatre, promising to be quick so his bros can have their turns.

He sneers, slaps a calloused hand hard across his ten-minute girlfriend's ass, and assures both the Lusthogs and the audience there won't be any foreplay.

No mercy in love or fucking. Even less in killing.

The Lusthog pursuit of the sniper is one of the tensest scenes in *FMJ* and was arguably designed with the intention of illustrating the metaphors of valor, vainglory, situational heroism, and the like. Animal Mother, Rafterman, Joker, and Donlon patrol a multi-story pile of rubble that is burning and collapsing all around them; if the pithy aphorism "War is Hell" holds any weight, this is its visual accompaniment.

Animal Mother and Donlon are out of view for the majority of this scene. It focuses on Joker, who moves with the caution of a little boy playing hide-and-seek in the darkness of a friend's grandmother's basement. Does he really want to find anything?

Despite his ginger approach, Joker makes a mistimed noise. The sniper, a Vietnamese girl who is about the same age as the prostitutes, wheels around and opens fire, causing Joker to drop his rifle. As he fumbles for his sidearm, terrified, Joker ducks behind a column. As he retreats, Rafterman comes from behind and pumps rounds into the sniper, dropping her. Rafterman is elated:

"We got the sniper!" he shouts, summoning the rest of the squad. Animal Mother, the first to respond, stands astride Rafterman and the still-shaking Joker. Rafterman asks if putting one through the sniper makes him a bona fide hard ass, but that's not the real question.

As the squad prepares to move out, Joker asks:

What about the sniper? He stands pointing down at the wounded girl.

She is panting and mumbling something in Vietnamese.

Animal Mother answers with his eyes: What about her? She's a fucking gook sharpshooter. Rat food, new guy. Fucking rat food. Let's roll out.

We can't, Joker says.

Donlon points out that the girl is praying. Praying to die. Suddenly her English improves:

In a series of raspy, choked whispers, the sniper begs to be shot.

Animal Mother, sensing Joker's dilemma, eggs him on:

You wanna? Go on. Shoot her.

It's the crisis that all of *Full Metal Jacket* has built up to. Is Joker a writer or a killer? Is he a puke, or a Marine? On the firing range, Hartman tells us it takes a hard heart to kill. But what if the gentlest action is to put a round between a young girl's eyes? Isn't Animal Mother—the steeled veteran grunt—the hardest of the lot? The biggest swinging dick? He looks down and sees the enemy who wasted his bros. She deserves nothing but pain and disdain. It is neither bullet nor Marine that will kill this mama san. If it is left to time, filth, and vermin. So be it.

Joker is the only one left with no blood on his hands. He still has access to his civilian humanity—it's in one of the pockets of his fatigues, maybe, and he can still take it out at night and shine a flashlight on it, remember it as it was and might be again—but at his feet is a door that, once opened, will never shut again.

The girl's pleading does not cease. Joker draws his pistol and agonizes for what feels like longer than it is, before squeezing a favor out of the gun and into the sniper's body.

You're fuckin hardcore, now, Donlon tells Joker.

Is this a compliment or a curse? Information or a judgement? In Shit World, does it matter? There are the living and the dead. Ghosts and suppositions are homeless and needless.

Joker has seen a living thing up close and killed it; even if it was the enemy, it was a human, a woman. In the catch-22 of *Full Metal Jacket*, this doesn't cheapen the kill, but pins it like a medal to Joker's persona. Face-to-face, close range, shot that bitch. He is nothing he believed he was, and also everything, because of what he's done here. Every stone and particle of dust that comes under his boot will be smaller now, crushed finer under the weight Joker carries[6].

---

[6]Yes, this is a nod to Tim O'Brien. I'll never be a Vietnam vet, a Harvard grad, or a writer of his caliber. I will be a thief with a conscience. Thanks, Tim.

No more female bodies appear in *Full Metal Jacket*, but there is one noteworthy allusion: Ann-Margret. In the *Stars and Stripes* field office, there're scuttlebutts about the sex symbol coming to visit. Rafterman, one of our mediators between the film and the females, is assigned to cover her arrival.

Lockhart, the CO of the journalism outfit, gives his photographer specific instructions:

Get some upskirts. Don't make it obvious, but get it done. Rafterman is his own kind of sniper on his own high-priority solo assignment: shoot the famous lady's lady parts and bring home the proof.

Much going on here yet precious little. Ann-Margret; at least she gets a name. She is also the only actual female character—a true life, Swedish-American actor and singer.[7] But she's not sacred, by any means. She's reduced to a metonym: a pussy. If she had the sex parts of a drill sergeant she'd be of no interest whatever, but the babymaker—the *boom boom* factory—that makes her at least worth objectifying.

Ann-Margret never shows up, though. As forecasted by Joker, the Tet ceasefire is violated and U.S. embassies are overrun by the North Vietnamese, as are other major points of control like Khe San.

---

[7] I had to look this up, I cannot tell a lie. According to the internet, she's been married to the same man since '67, making the vulgarities about her ironic. For all the leg she showed and the buzz she generated, she seems pretty wholesome after all.

Joker asks: does this mean no Ann-Margret?

There goes Joker, mouth before brain, getting himself shipped to Phu Bai and the real war, with no dirty pictures to console him.

Conflation is the only word I can find to describe the remainder of invisible women populating this Kubrickian space. Your sister, my sister, somebody's sister; she's all over the place, getting boned or bargained for by everyone from Hartman to Joker to Cowboy.

When Joker earns his moniker at boot camp, Hartman welcomes him to the fold by telling him his honesty is a damn fine trait. Maybe, Hartman says, he and joker should be friends. Better still, maybe Joker should come by one weekend and get horizontal with the Drill Instructor's sister!

Then he gut punches Joker and hovers over him, shouting him down and portending the ass-whippings and PT to follow. But Joker, instead of breaking, thrives within the torture and manages a chameleon's style of coping; as he and Cowboy mop the head, Joker breaks the silence with:

"I wanna make a trade to pork your sister."

"What've ya got?" Cowboy counters.

This is long before they banter with whores in Vietnam, but they are well versed in callousness already. Or maybe, I have to hope, they see through Hartman's abuses and know them for what they are—attempts to expel sensitivity where there isn't room for it. Joker doesn't know Cowboy's sister, if he has one at all. Cowboy doesn't mind the bro chatter, even if he's got six sisters. It's all bullshit, isn't it? It's Kubrick's equivalent of soldiers fawning over pictures of each other's gals in other war films.

Cowboy and Joker's love triangle with the unseen sister carries over to the fighting. When Joker finds Cowboy in the field, in the second act of the film, they fall right back into it:

COWBOY: You been getting any pussy?

JOKER: Only from your sister.

COWBOY: You're missing out cause she's not as good as my mom.

They embrace. It's legit tenderness, brotherly love. All the blood porn and sucky-fucky braggadocio aside, these men are happy to know one another. Whoever's sisters and mothers they've been dreaming of humping, I'm glad they had them, even if it turns out she was my mom too.

*

I don't remember Mom's first yeast infection, but they were common. Some of my earliest memories are of Monistat boxes and my mother stuffing bags of frozen peas between her legs.

"Be glad you don't have a cooter, Andrew," she'd say, and I was. Still am. Always and forever will be, world without end. She was plagued by irregular periods, urinary tract ailments, ovarian polyps[8], and of course, yeast infections.

I was sleeping off a good drunk on the sofa when Mom came in and slapped my cheek with the belt of her pink terrycloth robe. It was early, baby splinters of sunlight weaseling through the miniblinds.

"What?" I said. "Fuck's sake, what time is it?"

"I itch . . . down there."

I rolled over and threw my leg onto the back of the sofa. Pussy problems generally equaled simple discomfort and a good bit of whining. In the months since Dad's death, I'd learned this.

"It's got me worried. I think maybe I should go see Dr. Levy."

"You been pissin' razor blades all my life, woman. You're fine and you know it."

She paused and it was long enough for me to feel her panic, a contagious heaviness that came from the ceiling and slipped over Mom's shoulder, down her arm flab, to the wrist that would be surgically rebuilt eight years from then, into her fingertips that wiped herself after using the bathroom and

---

[8]It doesn't matter that the ovaries aren't in the vagina or even in the nether region in general; around my house, anything pertaining to or tangentially related to something pertaining to female reproductive equipment was a part of the vagina. "Your mother's having pussy problems," could mean anything from cervical cancer to PMS to a shy bladder.

accidentally found a wart on her thigh. Heaviness spared me the details, but there was a story it told.

"Andy, I'm afraid."

"I know."

"What if . . ."

"I'm up, woman, I'm up. I'll call the doctor. And when he prescribes an over-the-counter suppository I'm going to be pissed."

And relieved. I accidentally-on-purpose forgot to say relieved.

I think I knew. About the girlfriend, I mean.[9] Not who she was—or if it was limited to one—but I knew the old man was stepping out. I didn't care as much as I should've, partially because I blamed my mother.[10] But no, on the other hand,

---

[9] I was just sitting down to watch porn on the desktop PC I shared with my dad when I saw Match.com in the browser history. I wasn't on it, making the process of elimination real simple. I opened the page and saw: *Welcome back, Dutchman73! Sign in to see your newest matches!* That blinking cursor in the password field. I wanted to try it, see if I could guess the philandering fuck's passcode to online infidelity. I ached to know if it was something ironic like Mom's initials and her birthday, or something corny like "Loverboy." I didn't want to know, I wanted everything but. I wanted there to be no secrets to learn. Let my father be unknowable. I went to my favorite free porn site. The first vid on the homepage was a three-minute clip titled "*Cheating Husband Dominates Teen.*"

[10] A childhood spent being felt up by her grandfather made Mom dread men and not care a lot for sex. Pop probably tried to understand

fuck that. For all the old school stereotypes my father was happy to be, Loyal Husband shouldn't have been hard. His own parents had stayed married through five kids, three drinking problems, the Korean War, Richard Nixon twice, and leaving the three-story Folk Victorian on Virginia Avenue for a ranch style beige box across from the St. Cecilia greenhouse. What was bad enough about Mom and Dad's marriage that bringing in a lover was necessary?

---

that, if for no other reason than to talk Mom into the sack. He must've figured he'd solved all her problems when she really started trying to get pregnant and the "forced fucking sessions" started. In those days, Mom would hump the old man until his penis was raw. But then I showed up, a ten-pound baby who stole my mother's heart and my father's sex life. "Don't wake the baby." That's how it starts. Then it was "I've been home with the baby all day." Then: "What if Andrew comes in?" There were always excuses for not giving it up, and they were always anchored to me. I took my job—preventing my father from busting a nut—rather seriously in the end. Maybe it was some funky Oedipal thing; God knows the Freudians could make it so. But I really hated the way Pop would leer at Mom, the way he'd goose her when she did the dishes or how he'd cup her breasts from behind when she was brushing her teeth. I remember Mom's yellow pajama shorts and the way Dad's motor-oil fingers would try to wander up their legs or down their waistband. In front of me, in front of Mom's mother who lived in our house, in front of Button the German Shepherd mix. Shamelessly, pervishly. And when she'd slap his hand away, he'd yank her by the waist and say: "I paid good money to do that." And he'd smirk like he was joking and we all knew he was not. The price of being a stay-at-home mother in the early '80s was being a call girl married to your john; my mother was also Hooker number one.

I thought about that while I read *Golf Digest* in the gynecologist's waiting room.

"Is this your first?" an old voice asked. "Sir?"

"Oh, sorry, what?"

"Is this your first?"

The old woman smiled and her dentures were pristine. If only I knew what the fuck she was talking about.

"I don't follow," I said.

"Your first baby."

"Oh, no, I'm not here with my wife. My Mom's seeing the doctor."

"Oh," she said. She was clearly disappointed. "Well why did you have to come if it's your mother who's pregnant?"

"She's not pregnant, ma'am, she's seeing the doctor for something else."

"What else could she be seeing him for? He's a baby doctor."

I can feel myself regressing—the tension in my shoulders and the roiling in my belly, the drill sergeant's son becoming his father in defense of his mother. This woman reminded me of my neighbor Evelyn who used to babysit me, and yet she was going to get a dressing down for asking an innocent question. I'm sorry she couldn't read my body language. She was about to watch a movie instead—her own private screening of *Full Metal Jacket*, with me as the star and my father's long shadow as the director.

"You're not pregnant and you're here, what's your fuckin' story?"

"Oh!"

There was no stopping this now.

"Yeah. You're probably all dried up down there, but here we sit. What's your excuse?"[11]

Her daughter was knocked up and she was along for the ride because they were going to lunch and get "a brand new brasserie" after the daughter had her checkup. Of course.

"Well he's here with me because I've got crotch crickets and if my husband wasn't dead I'd kill him," Mom said.

I hadn't seen her come out. She stared down at the old lady like she was daring her to fight. Then she looked at me, her eyes puffing.

"I have herpes and I need a doughnut."

We marched, heads up, chests out, to the door.

"And mind your fuckin' business next time!" Mom barked over her shoulder.

She sobbed in the car. We were baffled. Mom had only been with Dad, and Dad had only been with . . .[12]

There were a bajillion follow-ups at the GYN after Mom's diagnosis. Sometimes there was a laser involved—like tattoo removal, but for genital warts. Other times there was a

---

[11]I've always wanted to go back to this moment and have her ask "Excuse for what?". That way I could be Hartman and drill it into her that I'm asking the fuckin questions here.

[12]We do not speak of this, Mom and me. She doesn't need it on top of everything else. And there's a chance I'm wrong. I'm not, but I could be, and "could be" is enough.

topical freezing ointment, and still other times just a simple straight pin. The growths went away, they came back. We left the doctor's office, we returned. My mother's lady region was a hotbed of suspense, and our favorite inside joke. She'd be in the bathroom and I would tap on the door:

"Everything okay?"

"Yeah, I'm going pee. Why?"

"Thought I heard crickets chirping."

"Fuck you, Andrew."

I lived with the queen of Kubrick's Full Metal Females, alone. My father was faithful to the gun, if nothing else. He got wasted and now I was running the squad.[13]

---

[13]Radio transmission to the old lady at the OBGYN:

Silver Bird, this is Trigger Happy Offspring, over. Silver Bird, do you read me? Over. You're right, it's time to retire the tone of the movie. It's tough when you're steeped in a particular tradition, though. Please try to understand that. I've been surrounded by strong women and weak men all my life and I'm trying to create a new normal. My dad and his idols went straight to violent outbursts and ballistic diction when they were hurt, scared, or trying to communicate. "Fuck" was one of the first words I learned. You didn't know you were poking a mine with your toe; I know this. So when I blew up, you were blindsided. Maybe I was too. Maybe I didn't know I could do it. Hurt you. Sound off like I had a pair. Be my father or who my father thought he was or wanted to be. Maybe I thought all that rage would stay inside and I'd keep it like the old man did. I don't know. Truly, I don't know. My mother was ashamed and uncomfortable, I was ashamed and uncomfortable. You were nosy and obtuse. I wanted to bring you into the fold—to embarrass you and make you want to crawl under the earth and not come out until you were sure I was gone. And for a long time I was convinced I'd done right. I'd done my duty. But what if you'd been my grandmother and I'd watched someone like me thrash you? I'd have killed him or wanted to. I don't know what I'm saying. A lot, that's for sure. But not very much at all. My father would've tried everything to get out of taking Mom to the doctor that day. He would have had me do it, even if he was alive. I was angrier with him than with anyone or anything that day. I didn't know that until . . . well, now. Or always.

Epiphanies are cute, aren't they? Another thing my father would never do: apologize. My mother didn't raise my father but she did raise me.

I'm sorry Silver Bird. And believe me, it hurts.

THE EMPATHY EXCISIONS

ONE

> "I am thinking a lot about empathy these days—
> defensively, I might add . . ."
>
> Phillip Lopate, "The Limits of Empathy"

I also find myself considering the existence and/or substance of The E Word, not simply because I enjoy having a thing in common with Lopate (though I do), but because of what I feel is a strong case against it.

Partially, my objection is semantic. Now, I admit this is slippery stuff since we exist not in a lexicographical vacuum, but in a dynamic and subjective perceptual arcade. However, there's a misnomer epidemic sweeping the English-speaking world (this is the only one I speak for with confidence, but it might translate into other tongues as well). Namely, we tend to say "*empathy*" when we mean something else. Lopate rightly asserts that usually the word we should use is "*sympathy*." This is true more often than not, as we shall see, but I think it's fair to posit that we also tend to confuse The E Word with "*compassion.*"

The American Heritage Dictionary defines compassion as:

"A deep awareness of the suffering of another coupled with the wish to relieve it. See synonym at: Pity."

I think that's what most of us mean by empathy; we don't mean what Phillip Lopate calls the "stickier, more ghoulish . . . delusion that one can actually . . . fuse with another's feelings." Most of the time, we mean to convey to the suffering individual a sense of visibility. Much of our language is meant for the purpose of extinguishing feelings of isolation, to bring others into a protective circle of shared humanness.

Sympathy does this too in its purest forms. Feeling sorry *for* someone. This is raw, uncomplicated sympathy, which is a knee-jerk emotion for me. While watching the World Series this year, for instance, I was elated for the Houston Astros (Jose Altuve is five-and-a-half-feet of pure joy to watch), but I was bummed for the Dodgers. As the cameras panned across the LA dugout, the disappointment and anguish were written on the faces of the losing team. I felt bad for them, felt sorry. But I didn't empathize—I didn't feel sorry *like* them. That's where empathy fucks up everything.

"Empathy: The act of understanding . . . and vicariously experiencing the feelings, thoughts, and experience of another of either the past or present without having the feelings, thoughts, and experience fully communicated in an objectively explicit manner."

(Merriam-Webster Online)

Being a compassionate fellow, I started talking to the Dodger players on the TV screen.

"Keep your head up," I said. "It's only a game. You'll get 'em next year. You had a hell of a season . . ." et cetera and. I knew they couldn't hear me, which was a good sign. I hadn't come off the rails entirely, although I am still young and the world is strange. Point being, I wished there were some cathartic, long-distance, pain balm I could send the crestfallen guys who'd just experienced the penultimate baseball defeat.

That's where compassion makes a hard left away from The E Word; compassion is accompanied by a desire to relieve someone's pain. The E Word just wants to feel it, commandeer it, be kin to it. True empathy would be the ability to look at the Dodgers (we're going to stick with the innocuous-seeming baseball analogy for a while, but it's far bigger than that. Imagine a funeral (or the immediate aftermath of a cancer diagnosis) and know *exactly* what kind of bad each player was feeling.

Maybe one of the starting pitchers had money on the game, a la Pete Rose.[14] For him, losing is a whole other kind of catastrophe. Let us imagine the second baseman promised a dying boy he would let him see a real World Series ring. That's another heartache, nuanced and layered. Every man on that team was crushed for his own reasons—or was he?

---

[14]Before the defamation speak begins, I'm not saying this is the case. If you were empathizing with me, you'd know that. See how that works? Impossible, isn't it? It's almost like I know something.

Maybe one of the Dominican players only feigned being miserable. If we can see him signing his first multi-year, huge-money contract, maybe we can also hear him thinking: *It's cool. I lost the game but I get to keep the paycheck.* The E Word would know this, in its totality, without any help from empirical data.

With the requisite apologies to true believers in empathy, I call bullshit. To believe this is possible is arrogant enough offend even the most caring individual. Empathy is founded on self-centeredness, by necessity. We first engage with the world and everyone in it through the lens of what we've experienced ourselves. No matter how worldly we are, we're only ever ourselves. To assume we can effectively become anyone else—nevermind *everyone* else—is the most egregious self-aggrandizement there is.

My old man used to do this. Whatever trauma or malady was affecting someone, Pop knew what they were feeling. Somehow my mother's irritable bowel syndrome was likened to the time Dad had diarrhea at Boy Scout camp in 1964. That Mom's condition was chronic (and exacerbated her also-chronic anxiety) and sometimes led to rectal bleeding was irrelevant. Pop was inexorably convinced he understood his wife's problems and, therefore, any of her attempts to communicate their severity or their accompanying needs were unnecessary.

He'd do it to me too, of course. Equal opportunist that he was.

A lifetime ago, I was a runner. This is not to exaggerate or create some dramatic effect; I'm thirty-four and this happened when I was seventeen. A lifetime ago. I had no raw talent, *per se*, but I was determined to prove that an asthmatic who was built more like a wrestler than a distance runner could cut the mustard. By the time I was a junior in high school, I was running Varsity Cross Country. We went to the State Meet that year in the Missouri state capital of Jefferson City. It was ninety-four degrees in November and the race was fast. Too fast. I was holding up well until the last quarter mile.

I ran into a fucking pole. Simple as that. Every other pole marking the course was a breakaway proposition—hit it and it would bounce away from you, then back up. Not this last one. It was cemented into the ground. I hit it, it hit me back. I'm not sure how long it took for me to stagger up, fall back down, then crawl to the finish line. But I know I made it across by dragging myself. I passed out, came to, and puked. I finished ninetieth out of two hundred and twelve.

I remember Dad standing over me, like Hartman would've done, and almost drowning me with Gatorade.

"Drink, goddamn it," he kept saying. "Drink."

In an hour I was woozy and ten pounds too light, but I was alive and walking around.

"I know what you're thinking," Pop said, looping his fat left arm around my neck.

"Oh?"

"You're thinking about how you let your team down. About how you could've broken your personal best time. You're thinking about the glory that comes with tearing off your fingernails to keep from being a quitter."

"I'm thinking I still finished in the top half, actually," I said.

"Because you didn't quit."

"Because the other guys were slow."

"Listen," Dad said. "It's like when I was still playing football . . ."

Again with the spurious connections between my life and my father's. He went on to tell me some story about how his school lost to another school, but in the last ten seconds they avoided getting shut out by scoring a touchdown.

"What's that got to do with me?"

"Everything. Don't you get it?"

"I think I'm gonna throw up again."

"Do it now, before we get in the car."

These empathies were clumsy and unfortunate but they weren't as insidious as others. My old man's empathy was, like a lot of other people's, rooted in benign logical fallacies. Perhaps it was even well intentioned. (Recall the old saw about what paves the road to Hell?) I'm willing to believe that about the vast majority of would-be empaths: they are guilty of minimizing, by accident, the suffering they're trying to share. Empathy wants to be misery's company, and sometimes it just . . . isn't. But there are tragic empathies.

For my father, the real cancer of The E Word came in subliminal waves borne from the TV.

Lopate writes:

"I saw that my attempts to explain myself were perceived as inappropriately 'academic,' therefore cold, therefore removed from emotions . . .."

Have I spent enough time in my head that I've philosophized this? Have I become the academe? Thus far, perhaps, I have painted with a brush made of pieces of the parietal lobe. I will enlist a sharper scalpel now, and bleed from deeper down. Temporal; aren't we all.

TWO

I spend a lot of time thinking
about_____:

". . . how empathy may just be narcissism
projected onto others;"

From Raymond Carver's OkCupid profile,
edited by Gordon Lish

R. Lee Ermey's first line of dialogue in Full Metal Jacket is an
introduction. He's the one in charge. The Drill Sergeant.
Closest thing to an almighty being there is on Parris Island.

That's what got Dad. First line, first viewing, forever had
him hooked. Dad was a retention counselor, yes. But before
he'd gotten as old and as fat as he'd ended up, he too was a
drill instructor. The obvious disparity between a USMC
recruit gunny and a Staff Sergeant in the National Guard
evaporated as the film unfolded. My father saw himself, felt
himself, heard himself in Hartman.

When I was much younger and first saw the movie, Pop
would make me sit next to him on the sofa, ramrod straight.

"This is how it is," he'd half-whisper. "This is the fuckin-
a real deal."

My "how would you know" reflex was still undeveloped,
so I believed him. R. Lee Ermey was, in fact, a Marine in
Vietnam. He served with Wing Support Group 17 and was in
Nam for 14 months. He was the first retiree in the history of

the Corps to receive a promotion.[15] But my father wasn't any of those. The empathy and kindred feeling he had for Ermey's fictional Drill Instructor trope was over-inflated. While Gunny Lee was shaping combat Marines, Dad was just yelling at weekend warriors—scaring kids for the sake of scaring them.

Learning to tie my shoes was a shitshow. I was a left-handed child of right-handed parents. My mother had the patience to teach me, but not the know-how. My father had neither, but he was my senior drill instructor and not my dad.

"You will square your ass away and affix those fuckin' shoes to your feet with double knots, and you will do it fucking now."

[Affix. Fancy word for tie? I am four here, Dad. I know what it means by the context clues, though I can't call them that yet. I also know you're changing registers—usually you'd just say "Put your fuckin shoes on, boy"—to mindfuck me. You don't know I know this and I will never tell you because, even once I'm grown, I will remain a little bit afraid. But then you'll die and I'll be braver than brave. Crazy and out loud. You will not see but I will do. Who says we should have no secrets from each other?]

In *Full Metal Jacket*, the recruits are terrified into all sorts of things they didn't think they could accomplish. They climb ropes, they run half-marathons through the Carolina underbrush and across mud lakes. As Joker tells us: they're ready to chow down on human flesh and be happy for it. My

---

[15]Compliments of RLeeErmey.com.

father is my gunny. There is no time for me to be a maggot who doesn't pack the gear to serve in the shoe-tying world.

"I will motivate you!"

[Motivate. Create in someone the desire to perform a certain task; does not connote providing assistance or instruction. I am motivated, Pop. I just don't know what the fuck to do.]

This is pure Hartman— My father slipped into character as often as he needed to or had occasion for. As I fumbled around with metaphors like "make bunny ears and have the rabbit go under the fence, then lasso the bunny with your rope," Pop thrived. I was helpless and he was superior, not only in size and achievement, but in authority.

"You will learn this shit! I will teach you!"

Again, Hartman. The old man's capacity for fearmongering was sharper than his originality. He would slap my hands. Ridicule me for not knowing how to reverse my instincts and mimic his own muscle memory. [In the film Hartman slaps Pyle across the left cheek. Was that left or right, Harman demands. He slaps the right cheek. Again, was that left or right? Don't get it wrong, Private.

You checked out of the verbiage just enough to avoid admitting you were a plagiarist, didn't you, old man?]

He'd mock me, wait for me to cry. When I did cry, I was a bitch. A weakling. My mother's son.

When I eventually learned to tie the accursed shoes, there was no celebration. There was always a new skill I had not learned or a new attitude I was not supposed to have. There was war all the time. And my father, as Hartman promised he would be, was a conveyor of death.

*

How much of my home movie do I show you? The episodes are innumerable: me, standing at attention in the center of the living room. This is to ensure that my senior drill instructor has unimpeded access to both of my flanks, as well as my front and rear. A totalitarian can only succeed if it can surround what it wishes to conquer. My father, screaming. One of his favorite techniques was the impossible question.

"Do you understand me?"

"Ye—..."

"Shut up!"

OR

"Do you understand me?"

" . . . "

"Answer me motherfucker!"

"Ye—"

"Shut the fuck up!"

In some eardrum of one of the cortexes, my brain has a recording of Dad's Hartman voice. Its pitch and tenor, its bombastic baritone. Gunny Dad is motherfucking the ghosts of every mistake he ever thought I made, but it only registers as a sub audible trigger that shoots off rounds of tinnitus. This is to say I am numb but not deaf.

*

Pop had other pompous empathetic tendencies. He'd become Joker, for instance, when he drove through a sobriety checkpoint while taking me home from a high school dance.

State Patrolman: Evening Sir, how are you tonight?

Dad: I'm having fun. I don't drink but you can breathalyze me. You know you wanna.

State Patrolman: Had anything to drink tonight, sir?

Dad: A few Pepsis but they were spaced out over the night.

State Patrolman: Have a lovely evening, dickhead.

Dad: Back at ya.

Why he had to do it—be a prize-winning prick when it was easier not to—is beyond me. My old man's blustering, phony bravado, like Joker's, was more dangerous than entertaining. But he thrilled to it, felt it was his alter ego's duty to sound off in circumstances like that.

Retail clerks and restaurant servers got similar smartass treatment, but (it occurs to me now) that didn't have anything to do with The E Word. That was my father being an asshole. The E Word was, as it always is, situational—selective. Only when confronted by people in positions of legitimate authority did Dad's defensive Joker-empathy ignite. Empathy is also more a matter of posturing —especially in the case of empathy with fictional characters. If imitation is the highest form of flattery, then empathy of this sort is the most histrionic mimicry. The E Word doesn't change us; we change behaviors, our personas, our looks, our concepts of self. We bend until, if you are my father, you break.

THREE

"I never saw a wild thing sorry for itself. A small
bird will drop frozen from a bough without ever
having felt sorry for itself."

D.H. Lawrence

The most destructive symptom of empathy is the
manifestation of self-pity. If it weren't there would be more
happy empaths. If I considered myself empathetic, let's say,
and a friend of mine called to say they'd just won the Pulitzer
Prize, what would The E Word have me feel? Elation, pride,
self-assurance, achievement, relief, maybe some anxiety at
having to give a speech (do they make you give a speech when
you win the Pulitzer?).

But that's not what I would feel.

I love my friends to a fault, but I'd be jealous. Happy
they'd accomplished something grand, yes, but jealous all the
same. In bed that night I'd probably start rereading their work
in my head, although I'd hate myself for it. *Is it really that
good? It's not that good,* I'd think. I would keep this nastiness
for myself and maybe my bartender (probably not, my
bartender knows everyone I do) and I'd do my damnedest to
be congratulatory. Or I'd just be very quiet until my childish
temper tantrum was over, which in fairness, could be quite
some time.

Because that's not the way The E Word functions; it
feeds on badness. Give unto The E Word your miscarriages,

your divorces, your hurt feelings, your insecurity about your body. Give unto The E People your tears and your "Why does this shit always happen to me?" Let them see your bruises, your bloodstains, the places where you've come undone. That's what empathy wants. And when it gets what it wants, The E Word can become the plastic explosive of The E People's implosion.

*

If you want to know what my father looked like, watch *Full Metal Jacket*. I'm serious. Pvt. Leonard "Gomer Pyle" Lawrence, played by a 27-year-old Vincent D'Onofrio, is almost Dad's doppelganger. He's 6'3" and weighs two hundred eighty pounds; Pop was 6'2" and, until he gave up on himself, weighed two eighty-five. Glasses would be the biggest difference, but that's an easy fix. Dad loved to take those off and make The Face: the deranged, mouth-open, heavy-breathing, head-tilty face Pyle makes in the film, right before he offs himself.

"Hi, Andrew," Pop would say, leering at me.

When I was young, I'd just giggle nervously; even the film's co-writer Michael Herr acknowledges the film is darkly comedic. Then, when I got a little older and had some hair on my nuts, I'd join the act.

"Are those real bullets?" I'd ask.

Dad would answer with the size of the cartridges in movie: 7.62.

Then together we'd almost sing the title:

"Full. Metal. Jacket."

And by the time I was in my twenties and Dad was about to sneak off and die without permission, I'd look at him, apropos of nothing, and in my own Hartman voice, ask a version of Hartman's last question before going down:

"What's your damage, troop?"

In reply, Dad would turn slowly, auditioning for the right to keep the part, and make The Face. Or, in the final days, he'd just keep marching toward whatever away he was going into.

If you want to get a sense of what my old man was like, watch *Full Metal Jacket*. I repeat: I'm serious.

With the established similarities (both real and imagined) between Pop, Hartman, and Joker, there's no overstating the resemblance of Dad to Gomer Pyle. Their mannerisms: oafish, little-boy innocence, big-bellied clumsiness, perpetually not-quite-right clothing. At one point in the film, Joker tells Pyle he looks more raggedy than usual and admonishes him to tuck in his uniform shirt. Dad didn't believe in bathing unless it was a special occasion. Christmas Eve: shower. Awards banquet at the armory: shower. In the interim between soapy observances, he looked like shit. He used to carry a Maglite, a Leatherman multitool, and his cellphone all holstered to the right side of his belt; the result was a postural slump and his pants sagging off one side of his ass, exposing his BVDs. He looked, again, like shit.

*

Whiners, both of them, Pyle and my father.

The day before his blanket party, Pyle snivels to Joker. The whole squad hates him, he says, even the one man charged with helping him square away.

Joker says something tired, like *I'm doing my best* but not that.

If I believed in The E Word, I'd feel it for Joker right here.

Dad torpedoed our family finances several times before I was born. Every time, until the last big one, Mom rescued him.

"I told him "Give me all the bills and no matter how fucked up they are I won't be angry." And I'd sort us out, however long it took. Then, stupid me, I'd give him the reigns again. Finally, I just gave up. He wasn't going to be honest with me, and he never learned a thing. I just pretended I didn't know anything about anything. Turns out, I guess I didn't," she tells me.

I can see it. I can hear Pop stumbling and stuttering and bungling even a plea for help. He was—like Pyle—a fuck-up. And—like Pyle—he just kept getting caught at it. But Pop had so many competing empathies at work inside him that he was incapable of existing as any of the selves he took on. Hartman inhibited Joker but triggered Pyle, which was trumped at some point by Hartman again, which left no room for Jeff, who was everybody.

*

My father's name was Jeffrey Michael Smart. He was born February 27, 1955. He'd be sixty-two right now.

Vincent D'Onofrio was born June 30, 1959. Close enough to have gone to high school with Pop.

I wonder if Vince ever took any shit for his name, like his character did in the movie. Hartman tells us the surname Lawrence is for gays and the navy Dad knew that feeling. Smart. What a goddamn name to grow up with, especially if you're kind of dopey looking.

"People used to say things to me twice because they thought I was stupid," D'Onofrio told an interviewer about life while he was portraying Gomer Pyle. I said a million things to my father on a million occasions. I repeated myself over and over: Yes sir, no sir, fuck you, Dad. But I never told him I understood. I never empathized with him.

I couldn't. I can't. I don't.

*

The chief empathy of my father's life was with the victimization of Gomer Pyle. Nobody who's seen the movie more than twice can deny that Pyle is abused beyond reason. Nobody who's seen the movie as many times as me and my old man can argue that the other recruits don't demonstrate the transformation of young men into killers—Pyle's death is a psychic homicide, the suicide of someone who is tormented. Nobody who has ever even causally breathed The E Word can deny that Pyle was, from the outset, in a world of shit.

Pop felt this. Felt victimized, beaten on.

He used to cry about having been on the gifted track in junior high, about the burden and the expectation and how he carried the scars of being different even then. His father beat him, his mother didn't love him, his wife often thought about divorcing him, his son thought he was an ogre. A bar of soap in a towel might've felt like a massage behind that.

Dad found his shadow in Gomer Pyle. He could watch himself be brutalized by circumstance and other people, and he could just sit still and feel it. Dad's empathy for Pyle began upside down like everything we see, and then the rods and cones of his steely eyes inverted the image and gave them to his brain. From there they ingratiated themselves to a long held but dormant self-pity. And then it was decided.

*

Vincent D'Onofrio didn't know he was my dad because he's not. Vincent D'Onofrio is alive, just like Gomer Pyle. All you have to do is rewind. If you want to make sure Pyle feels no pain, just don't watch the movie. But if you want to know my father in one of the most intimate ways I know him, you will watch. You will watch and you will not turn away. You will not turn away and you will not know what this means or what will become of you.

Andy Smart

You will, for a couple of hours, lose everything.

You will have empathy with silence and it will haunt you.

FOUR

(Or, The Empathy Epistles)

[Andy]
Hey, did you get that thing I sent you about The E Word?

[Lisa]
Yup.

What'd you think?

I think you're a guy, and that's why
you think half of the things you do. Like a lot
of the empathy stuff. It's . . . male.

The fuck does being a guy have to do
with thinking empathy is bunk?

Uh, kind of a lot. You guys are fixers. Sometimes
that's not what a situation calls for, you know?
Like, sometimes we need a wallowing partner,
somebody to just sit with us and our
shitty feelings. Sometimes we need empathy.

I'm not following.

        I know. You're tripping over your penis.

C'mon, I'm serious here. Do you actually think
it's possible for someone to know exactly
how anybody else feels?

        Well, no, but is that the only thing holding you up?
                        Exactly?

It's a big goddamn holdup. It's
more presumptuous and douche-baggy
to think you can do that than it is to want to
make somebody's pain go away instead of just
being there.

                        Not really.

How not really? It cheapens you if I say
"I know how you feel." Because no, I fucking don't.
I can guess at it, and I can agree that whatever
bad shit you're going through sucks and that I wish
you weren't going through it.

I disagree completely. It points to how valuable
you think I am that you would try. But it cheapens
me when you say you wish I wasn't having whatever
painful or difficult experience I am, because everything
builds us into who we are meant to be.

Ok, besides the hippie bullshit involved there,
you just proved my point: it values you when
I TRY to know what you're feeling. And, I'm sorry,
it'll never be better for someone not to wish they could make
someone's pain go away. Sympathy, man. Even though
I know I can't make it better, I'll always want to.

I really think we're saying the same thing.

You just don't wanna be wrong.

I'm not wrong. We're both right.

THAT'S NOT HOW IT WORKS.

This, too, is a male line of thinking.
You should stroke your penis, or something.
It's making you look like an asshole.

Not a terrible idea, actually.
I may just do that.

                         See? I empathized with you, there.

NO, YOU SOLVED THE PROBLEM.
TOTALLY FUCKING DIFFERENT, LISA.

                                          Love you.

Only toddlers and teachers say penis.
Love you, too.

                Just because your dad didn't empathize with you
                    the way he did with the movie shouldn't skew your
                            whole opinion of empathy as a concept.

I won't argue it should, but I'll tell you
that it does. It was toxic, it was warped, it was,
ultimately, fatal. I don't blame the flick, but
The E Word can kiss my entire ass. Cheek by fleshy
cheek.

What about Leslie Jamison? You read *The Empathy Exams*, right.

I'm waiting for the audiobook. I think her voice might help me enter the emotive realm of her related experiences and perceptions.

You are a prizewinning prick sometimes, Andrew.

Decidedly. Anyway, I gotta get back to work. Call you tomorrow?

K.

You're not pissed at me are you?

No, not at all.

PSYCH, I ALREADY KNEW THAT!

*

I call my mother and inform her that her ex-officio-daughter-in-law thinks my dick is impeding my thinking parts re:

empathy. Does Mom believe in empathy, or does she, like Phillip Lopate's favorite people, "operate out of a moral code older than empathy"?

"I don't know, sweetheart. I think that's a lot of words for pretty much the same thing. I wouldn't let yourself get worked up about it."

"But do you think Dad . . ."

"I think your father is dead and that we've got plenty of better things to think about."

"Like what?"

*

Dear Dad—

I was going to try and recreate the inside of the Father's Day card I dropped in your casket, but I can't remember what it said. If you get a chance, open it up and maybe let me know. I don't know what the fuck I'm doing here, what exercise in futility I'm indulging myself. But I wanted to say I'm sorry. Do you remember that one time when I was little? I was sick again, and you brought me orange juice without me asking. I barfed it all over myself and Mom was thunder-pissed at you. I guess the Doc said only clear liquids. But you just knew how much I loved OJ and you wanted to do something nice for me. I'm sorry it backfired, Pop. I am really sorry everything backfired. Everything, always.

The More You Hate Me

*

[Andy]
I wrote my Dad a letter last night.

[Lisa]
Oh yeah? What'd it say?

I don't really wanna talk about it.

Okay, that's fine. But, then
why'd you bring it up?

::shrugs:: I guess I just wanted somebody to know.

A NUMBERS GAME

My symbol of a soldier will always be my dad, but that of the Missouri Army National Guard is a militiaman with a musket at his hip. Beneath him is the credo: *"Always ready. Always there."* The symbol of the 1138th Engineer Company is a mounted knight on a golden horse; his sword is pointing like Babe Ruth's bat into some outfield and victory.

At a writer's retreat somewhere in the Ozarks, a pot smoking poetry proctor asked me: *"What is the symbol of your people?"* It's curious to me that I didn't say either the bronze man or the gold horse, either the gun or the sword; that I didn't claim the radar tower outside my father's barracks, or the F-16 with shark teeth that Dad said would provide air support if I was ever in trouble. I didn't pick the poppies Dad got from the bank every Veteran's Day, or the First Sergeant's Major Achievement Award he had framed and hung in the living room. I didn't pick his boot knife, either, or anything violent.

I chose 1138 without thinking. It's one, two, three, or four numbers, depending on the day. But 1138 is also a shadow of my father standing on the tarmac of an airport telling me to take care of my mother. It's the cool underneath the branches of the dogwood tree where Dad laid down to die. The number is a time, a place, a sensation. It's a window through which I stare in at myself when I was undamaged. I sleep with and under 1138, I wear it in my night sweats like my father wore his dog tags and my mother wears her wedding ring.

In Roman numerals, 1138 looks like this: **MCXXXVIII**

Under my eyes, it looks like fatigue.

On the page, it is a dragon in the uncharted seas of old maps.

*

Child Andy Remembers:

The old man's unit in the National Guard was the 1138th Engineers. I remember the armory at Jefferson Barracks: the long white building where Staff Sergeant Daddy had his cubicle—the GI desk that looked like it was stolen from the set of a low-budget documentary about public school principals or from a film noir detective's office, the bulletin board with fliers from recruiting and retention events three years before still push-pinned to it, the chair on casters that squeaked like a stepped-on kitten, magazines and Pepsi cans overflowing the trash basket, the smell of cigarettes and Mennen aftershave, young soldiers saluting as they became silhouettes in the doorway before moving out and leaving echoing footfalls, a tall black soldier the next spot over offering me root beer.

Adult Andy Knows:

The old man's unit in the National Guard became the 1035th Maintenance Company several years before Dad died. 1138 moved to Farmington, a Podunk outpost nearly an hour south of St. Louis. They were activated for duty in the Gulf; Dad and the 1035 were sent to Germany to repair old tanks. He brought me back a beer stein and some French cigarettes. He brought mom chocolate and *Kinderwein*.

Pop deployed to Europe twice for a month at a time when I was in high school. Then 9/11 came. If war had ensued right away, he'd have fought and I would have too. Our rage was fresh, our patriotism dumb and raw. But by the time the offensives in Afghanistan and Iraq began, Dad's political machinery had begun to work. He was old. Too old for that shit, for sure. And besides that, he couldn't back George W.

My father retired from the service in Winter of 2001. I remember the ceremony; Pop standing tall before a General who was younger than him, receiving a handshake and a brass medal that in military speak read: Congratulations, you can no longer hack it. His boots were shiny for their last inspection.

*

11:38am, yesterday, almost four thousand days since Dad's death.

I am sweating and my boxers are knotted around my nuts. My comforter is on the floor and the tower fan on the nightstand is blowing in my face. Mucus drains down my throat. I look at the time and wonder what I was dreaming about before all this. I wonder what sorcery or sleepy time voodoo jolts me awake at this hour at least three times a week. I wonder why I haven't found a job yet that makes me wake up before noon. Perhaps it would alleviate the ghost clock problem.

I do not believe this.

11:38pm, yesterday, the end of the almost-four-thousandth-day since Dad's death.

The lines on the highway are blurring together in the rain. I've got no windshield wipers, no driver's side mirror, and a photosensitivity to oncoming headlights. Pop parallel parked a Humvee once at the armory. He could manage this now, better than me. He used to tell me "sometimes you've gotta say FIDO; Fuck It, Drive On." Fuck it, but I'd rather pull over and call my dad for help. I pray to the lesser gods of traffic instead.

*

1138

Eleven is a Master Number.

If ten is order in the universe, eleven is chaos. If ten is purity, eleven is sin.

*

1138th on 12/21/92

Again the white building, again the barracks. But this time, the basement. A long room, a gymnasium. Buffet dinner in chafing dishes, paper plates sectioned into threes to keep Daddy's mashed potatoes from contaminating his noodle salad or mostaccioli. I have a roll that Mom buttered for me. After I eat, I chase Kirk Darling's daughter around the gym. She wants me to kiss her under the mistletoe, but there isn't any and we wouldn't know it anyway. We are eight years old.

When we leave the party, I am sweating in my short-sleeved dress shirt and I have cake on my tie. Daddy is angry with me about this, Mom is angry with him about something else, and I am angry at Kirk Darling for having a daughter.

Mom throws an orange that I didn't know she had at the building. Daddy says she threw it at him. They scream outside the car in the cold. Inside the car they are quiet.

*

It will be Christmastime again soon and my father is not here. My mother is eating an orange in the living room and watching a true crime program on TV.

*

1,138 days ago.

You are standing in line at the grocery store, waiting to buy beer and toilet paper. A man behind you is pushing his cart into your ankles and you wish he were dead. In front of you, there's a newspaper on the endcap. The headline reads: "Police Chief Issues Apology to Michael Brown's Family." Michael Brown is a young black man shot by a young white cop last month, and the riots following his death have not yet cooled. The man pushing his cart into your heels mumbles that Mike Brown was a porch monkey. You wonder what your father would've said, or if he'd have stared at the rubber conveyor belt and waited in silence. The man pushes his cart again, and you remember you wished he were dead, like Mike Brown and your father. You don't wish they were dead (you don't think you do) but they are, and you can't change it. The man is talking to himself as a way of talking to you.

"I wouldn't apologize to those niggers," he says. "Out there burning down their neighborhood. Don't see white folks pulling that crap when somebody dies."

The man is waiting. The wheels on his cart are full of potential energy. You want to tell him to back off. You want to make him back off. You wish you were your father because you realize now what he would do. He would become Hartman, the Gunnery Sergeant from Kubrick's *Full Metal Jacket*, your old man's favorite film. He would glare at the man after turning on him slowly, cinematically. The movie of your life would conflate the script and your old man's attempts at eloquence.

"To me, you are all subhuman morsels of day-old excrement," your father would say. "Pieces of shit," he would add as he paid for his groceries.

You set your beer and Charmin Extra on the conveyor. You step away from the man and his cart.

He follows you.

*

1138

Eight is my life path number. I have added the digits in my birthdate and amalgamated them into a single digit. The sum is indicative of my destiny to make a big splash in the world of money, control, power, and influence. But I have authority issues and can, when out of alignment, be a bully or blame others for the obstacles facing my eventual greatness. My life key is accepting that I am a born powerhouse.

I do not believe this.

*

The total number of words before this sentence is 1,138.

*

11 minutes, 38 seconds into *Full Metal Jacket*.

I freeze the frame and watch electrofuzz bisect the screen.

Play.

Gomer Pyle whimpers. His chipmunk cheeks puff out and collapse down like little loaves of punched bread. He is smarting from being slapped across both sides of the face for confusing his left and his right. In another second, Hartman will menace him:

Don't fuck with the Drill Sergeant. Not now, not ever.

But for this lone instant, the camera is trained only on his pinked flesh and his bruised humanity. It is as close to a film cell of my father as there ever will be and is eerily similar to the only photograph I have of him. For all the Hartman bluster, Pop was still a fat, scared recruit underneath.

*

1138

Three means lucky, fortunate. Three means unity.

Pythagoreans consider three the first real number because there are three sides of a triangle. Three triangles interlocked are a Viking symbol for the slain dead. Three naked men and a Latin epithet appear on the Nobel Prize.

Three means trinity: Father, Son, Holy Ghost.

Which of these is the hypotenuse? What do I square to discover it? How is the ghost of my father holy? Three questions. If I answer one, the other two become obvious.

In tarot, three is the card of the empress—the creator, the benevolence.

Christians believe their savior was dead and in hell for three days before being resurrected. My father has been dead much longer. Three does not work for my father.

*

1Z39

When I cry, these characters look like 1138. They are the coordinates to my father's grave—latitude 1Z, longitude 39. His is the white marble headstone that looks like everything else.

*

1138th at the Bungalow

It's the oldest beer garden in St. Louis and is a tremendously beloved shithole. You have been drinking here for two years, legally, four years total. You know the middle-aged prom queens who tend the bar, the lechers and dotards and cirrhosis-livered who come here, the ice in the urinals that doesn't quell the stink of piss and vomit. You are as much a fixture as the barstools here.

You see a man with biceps the size of your waist. His girlfriend is stripper-pretty and they are both blackout drunk. On his right forearm is a tattoo of a lightning bolt and the letters TCB. Takin' Care of Business. He falls into you while slap-fighting his woman.

"Sorry bro," he says. "Buy you a shot?"

"I'm alright, thanks," you say.

"Fuck that noise. Whiskeys! I'm still spending my Iraq money. Haji wants to buy me a whiskey!"

You are laughing and nervous. You are witnessing PTSD, you think.

"What branch of the service?" you ask.

"Army. 1138th Engineers. Fuckin Sappers. You know what they say? An engineer can be a grunt, but a grunt can't be an engineer! Twenty-one fuckin Bravo, best MOS on earth. You serve?"

"Not exactly. My old man was a drill sergeant in the 1138th when they were at JB."

"Fuckin-A! My fuckin bro!"

You toast your father, who is not dead yet, but alive and asleep. You stumble home from the tavern, buzzing with fermented fraternity. You have a new friend, a blood brother named Chance. You are trashed and you are happy. Streetlights have halos and you imagine they are grenades suspended in flight, just beginning to detonate. Everything is still except you, who barrels toward goodnight, but not gently.

"Semper Fi," you mutter to the dumpsters. "Be all you can be! Aim high! Join the Navy, see the world!"

You are vast. You contain multitudes. Do you contradict yourself? Very well. You contradict yourself.

When your father dies, Chance will take you to a 3 AM bar and get you puking wasted. A frat brother from a Catholic college will bump into you and apologize profusely but it will not stop Chance from choke-slamming him through a high table.

You will never be far from violence again.

*

11:28pm, tonight.

It'll come, whether I notice it or not, but I will because I'm waiting now. It's not always artificial, the noticing. My heart has an arrhythmia from alcoholism and smoking, but it is tripped too by time. I have two cardiac events per day. Eventually that will stop and I will be honorably discharged from the strange and sentimental business of existing. But in seven minutes my chest will go tight and I will know. Six minutes.

My phone goes off.

"Are you okay?"

It is my Lisa, my best-friend-turned-common-law-wife from Kansas.

"Yes," I type back.

Four minutes.

"It's coming."

"I know."

"I know you do."

*

1,138 steps.

You are dazed from want of sleep but not lack of fatigue. Your arms are goosebumped, your lower back tight. It is late, or it is early, or it is always. You leave the house and the air is an icicle overhead. The first breath stings, the second is mentholatum, the third you do not notice. You're moving without thinking, but you are thinking about something else; you are remembering your father's voice telling war stories he did not live through. He is braggadocious, grandiose. He is in a bar called the Ashau Valley, named after the battleground in Vietnam. You cannot see him or the other men who are staring at him in silence, but you can hear him. And you can hear them thinking, *This guy's full of shit.* Your father is Payback in *Full Metal Jacket*, talking about ops he wasn't in-country for. Where you are going now, there are dead who were killed living the life your father spun myths about.

Proceed as you are, north. A long chain link fence to your right, a sleeping German Shepherd guarding a used car lot. The tax attorney who called your father every day for a month to collect a past due bill lives a block up on the left. You cross the street.

Turn left into St. Matthew cemetery and follow the road toward the mausoleum with a Buddhist swastika on each of the front columns. Resist the urge to spit and remember it is a symbol of unity in consciousness. Instead, walk faster and feel the winter phlegm in your throat, hear a rattle in your lungs. Wheeze a bit in the brown grass as you veer off the road and toward the black marble bell marking your double-great-grandfather's grave.

Lean on the stone, feel its permanence and let it frighten you. You are in a field of cholera, consumption, tuberculosis, and simple despair.

But Ron Bozikis, who went to high school with your parents and was killed in Laos during Vietnam, is buried where you are walking, double-time, now. His headstone is still clean white decades on. His photo is still that of a smiling boy whose belly does not push against his uniform. Ron was an Army Ranger and volunteered to fight.

He looks nothing like your father.

You kneel and try to pray, or to say *"thank you for your service."* But you are not grateful or penitent, you are sleepy and cold and alone. You were a child once, even younger than Ron who is forever twenty-two, but you are not one now. You are a pedestrian on a one-way street being surveilled by the inevitable and the unwanted.

You stand. You leave the grass blades and dust on the knees of your jeans.

You have traveled one-half of three-quarters of one mile. As you begin to work backwards, out of death and into its prelude, you are less nimble. You shorten your stride, square your shoulders, and know the wind will be at your face this time.

You walk anyway.

You go home.

*

End Credits

The numbers 1,1,3, and 8 add up to 13. But the symbol of my people is not that number, the upside-down horseshoe, or a Born to Lose tattoo. It is not 7.62, the size of the bullet that gives *Full Metal Jacket* its name. It's not 6, 15, or 7, though together they make up the date my father died. My symbol for soldier will always be my father. In my naiveté, which comes and goes, Dad will always be standing in the doorway of our house in his BDUs, looking ready. Appearing there. The time on his GI wristwatch will always be 11:38. He will never die all the way; twice a day he lives for sixty seconds.

CINE FILES

Cinephile: Noun—a person who is fond of motion pictures (simplified):

My father loved nothing the way he loved the feel of his bare thighs on the cold Naugahyde cushions of the sofa—this meant he was pantsless and the TV was on.

Growing up, Channel 11 had a Sunday afternoon ritual that my father revered. Beginning at noon, there were six hours of movies with intermissions between that were long enough to pee, make a Tombstone pizza, and dispatch me to the basement fridge for a Pepsi. Sunday Movie One was usually an old western. It was *The Alamo* at least once a month, but Dad didn't care. He would watch whatever it was until he fell asleep with the TV Guide in his lap.

Toward the end of the first film, he'd snore himself awake and find that Sunday Movie Two's opening credits were rolling. The second flick was potluck—it could be *Big Trouble in Little China*, it could be *The Deer Hunter*. TV Guide was wrong more than it was right but you were obliged to watch if only to find out if you'd keep watching, which Dad always did. He'd have provisions by then, lunch and a snack and milk and a soda, and a Tom Clancy novel to read during the commercials. It was comical, the way he'd spread himself on the floor in front of the couch: long, hairy legs spread out and splayed open, all his accoutrements beside him, a tattered Army PT shirt with holes in the armpits covering his torso and doubling as a napkin.

He'd fall asleep during the second movie too because, for Dad, that's part of what most movies did: they lulled you away from the world so you could relax and rest easy. I wonder if he dreamt in film cells.

By the time Sunday Movie Three rolled around, Pop was as dressed as he'd ever be: jeans, a clean-enough t-shirt, and white tube socks with blue and yellow rings around the top. I think he primped thusly in anticipation of *Sixty Minutes* and Sunday dinner. Sunday Movie Three was the best of the lot because it aired during primetime and drove the network's Nielsen ratings. It was the most relevant, had the best cast, and was generally a drama.

I remember the Sunday it was *Platoon*. I was too young to realize how young Charlie Sheen looked in that movie, or to recognize Willem Dafoe or Tom Berenger. I didn't know it was an Oliver Stone movie, and if I had I wouldn't have known what that meant or why it mattered. All I knew was that there was a plethora of voiceovers where profanity once was, and that Dad offered this review at the end:

"It's no Full Metal Jacket."

*

Cinephile: noun—an individual whose passion for movies leads them to deeper appreciation of the art of filmmaking.

Here, my old man falls off the scent. He was a philistine and never apologized for it. There's a scene in *FMJ* where Hartman stands over Joker and shouts him down. The camera is situated in such a way that it's a true POV shot—we see Hartman through Joker's eyes. Stanley Kubrick was a cinematic pioneer, one of the first (*the* first according to some) to incorporate such camera work. I doubt Dad ever knew or cared about that. He also had no use for arthouse movies or the *avant-garde*; I tried to watch David Lynch's *Blue Velvet* with Dad and he lasted about twelve minutes.

"The fuck is this even about?" he asked.

"Watch the movie," I said. "Isn't that what you always tell me? Watch the fuckin' movie?"

"Yeah, but this is just weird."

"It's not as weird as *Eraserhead*."

"I have no child."

Pop also didn't give a rip about the basic lie movies tell: the action you are seeing and hearing was captured as is, *in media res*. There are months, sometimes, of principle photography before a film really begins being shot. Depending on the film, many of the sounds are artificial—a Foley artist in a studio is creating the sounds of dogs jumping into truck beds, doors slamming, helicopter blades thwacking the air. A lot of falsity goes into the realism of cinema. But, for audiences like my father, that was all irrelevant. What he saw was what happened, and what happened was what counted.

I took a film class in junior college after a booze-fueled semester of university. My professor, a playwright himself, recommended we read the original text of Denis Diderot's "The Paradox of the Actor" and try to explain it. I don't remember what I took from the essay then, or if I bothered to read it. Now, however, I've read it several times and I'm still only capable of distilling it into this:

It's just a movie. The actor is in character and, after the first few takes, doesn't feel the emotion of their character. Instead, an actor who can deliver the most command performance is in complete emotional control; they are outside themselves and are therefore able to become someone else.

Diderot is considerably more brilliant than I, and I may have done his treatise some disservice here. Overall, I think I've got the gist. My father never read Diderot, didn't know who he was. Pop was the kind of guy who, if I asked him if he was familiar with Diderot, would've said:

"Yeah, he was a backup jock strap washer for the Packers in '68. Mrs. Diderot's little boy."

I do wonder if my father considered what an actor thinks or feels. I wonder if he thought about Al Pacino in *Serpico*; if he imagined Pacino feeling the estrangement and ostracization of his character. Or if Pop imagined Vincent D'Onofrio feeling all the abuse and psychic decay of Gomer Pyle in *Full Metal Jacket*. He didn't live long enough to see Daniel Day Lewis portray Abe Lincoln, but I wish I could sit next to my father and watch him watch that movie. What would he see? Or who?

Cinephilia: noun—a condition of fascination with motion pictures which leads to the frequent or constant viewing thereof (simplified); the state of being transfixed by film at large or a single film and subsequently watching it repeatedly (standard); obsession with a movie that leads to it being played in your house with such regularity as to warrant your surviving son writing it down (disambiguation; colloquial).

It started with *North and South*, in 1985. A Civil War epic spanning four VHS tapes and starring Patrick Swayze and David Carradine. Sold to my father on Christmas. By mid-January, everyone in my house (excluding myself, I was two; possibly excluding my grandmother, she was going deaf; not sure about the dog—she was a German Shepherd and they're smart) knew every character and most of their lines.

Pop was obsessed with that film in part because he'd always identified as a Southerner. There's a tin photograph in the hallway between my living room and the kitchen; it hangs over the wooden foldout cubby where the phonebook used to live. It's a picture of me and my dad, side-by-side dressed in Civil War uniforms. He's a model of Confederate poise. Hell, he even kind of *stands* with a drawl. His sash is just right, his hat sits perfectly atop his head, and his revolver is aimed (I just noticed) at my temple. Pop's finger is on the trigger, the hammer is cocked, and he's serious looking but not somber.

I, on the other hand, am maybe nine years old. My jacket is too big—the cuffs are floppy and you can't see my chest—my hat is all catawampus, and I have it tilted way too far back on my head; otherwise I couldn't see a damn thing. My pistol is wrong, too, from a historical standpoint. It's a flintlock, more like those from Napoleonic battles. I have it aimed diagonally, holding it with both hands, so when fired it would rip my father's jaw off. Like Pop, I have my weapon cocked and my finger on the trigger. My face is sour, a boy trying to mimic a man.

I am wearing a Union infantryman's garb.

"I have no child," Pop said after the picture was taken. "My son would never be a Yankee."

Eventually *North and South* lost its luster and was replaced by other films. Dad was, more than anything, lazy. He grooved certain movie habits and didn't care enough to break them. *The Sons of Katy Elder*, for instance. Dad dug cowboys and had a manman crush on John Wayne meaning he watched that movie a hundred times. He knew what was coming and could let his eyes glaze over, nod off for a bit, and then yell at me for turning it off:

"I was watching that!"

"Sure you were."

"I was, I can tell you exactly where it was."

"No you can't."

"Turn it back."

"No, you're snoring so damn loud I can't even . . ."

"Boy . . ."

"Yes, sir."

He binged on *Shogun* because *bushido*, the samurai code of honor, was romantic to him. He watched *Working Girl* every night for two weeks because there's a halfway-decent sex scene (by Dad's standards; it's lame). He observed all of those, let them watch him as much as he watched them. But there was nothing anchoring him to any of these films, it was just Dad's ass on the sitting place and the spectacle of things.

Full Metal Jacket was different.

Full Metal Jacket was alive. Unlike my father, it still is.

A WORLD OF SHIT

The premise defines simplicity: follow a platoon of new Marine recruits from basic training into whatever comes next. As Hartman tells the recruits on their graduation day:

Most of today's graduates will be sent to Vietnam. Many of them will also not come back.

The inevitability of death, the tenuous nature of existence, the destruction and darkness of war; these are not new themes, not revolutionary content for writers, filmmakers, or consumers. Dad had done his time with war pictures, what was special about this one? The short answer: my father's guilty conscience and undeserved bravado, his insecurities and self-doubt. His need for a secondhand valor to replace his firsthand shame.

Pop missed Vietnam by a month. He turned eighteen in February 1973; the last troops pulled out in March. Too young to be drafted, too late to volunteer. Thus began my father's life of compensation.

*

My father sits alone in the living room with all the lights off. It is after midnight and he has just returned from work. There is grease from machine rotors and fan belts on his hands and face, which is flickered over by the TV. It is midway through the opening act of *Full Metal Jacket,* and my father has gone away. Gomer Pyle sucks his thumb and wears his cap backward while the rest of the platoon does squat-thrusts and counts them off with chutzpah. My father sits alone in the living room, being punished for an uncommitted sin.

*

I don't see my old man waiting in line outside the theater at Kenrick Plaza to get tickets for *FMJ.* I don't see him at the concession stand with a Coke and a box of Milk Duds, or a tub of popcorn. I see my father spending the summer of 1987 at work: the Post Office at night, the National Guard one weekend a month, and sometimes a side gig doing unarmed security for Wells Fargo.

I see Dad loping through his life. He'd been married for almost fourteen years by then and was the father of a three-year-old. When his life wasn't ennui, it was crisis; when he wasn't bending a wrench, he was dealing with my bedwetting. I could speak in whole sentences but I couldn't hold my bladder.

I remember watching Dad dress for work one day. He was buttoning his navy-blue work shirt and making sure his

Postal ID badge was clamped secure to his pocket. I was standing in the hall in my underpants.

"Excuse me, father," I said, walking into the bedroom, "would you kindly provide me with directions to the nearest local public library?"

He stared at the brass hardware on his dresser for a second, then looked at me.

"Sure. Go to Bates Street and go left. Go left on Eichelberger. It's on the right, before you get to Hampton. But you can't leave the house without a grownup and you can't cross any streets unless you're holding my hand."

"Okay."

I toddled back to whatever make-believe game I'd been playing.

"No more *Sesame Street* for the boy," Dad told Mom as he left the house.

It was that kind of domesticity that pained my old man. He craved better stories to tell than: "My kid wants to go to the library." While other men of his age brooded about war wounds, Dad had it soft. He worked hard, yes, and noble. But a mechanic is not a warrior, and that's what Pop wanted to be.

I don't see my father knowing where to find *Full Metal Jacket*. I see it coming to him. I see the two of us at Star Video on a Saturday. I am sick, because I often am, and Dad is off work and takes me to the allergist. I will be down for several days and we are stockpiling *Teenage Mutant Ninja Turtle* cartoons for medicine, when there it is: *FMJ* on VHS.

"That's a Daddy movie," Pop says. "It's about soldiers and stuff that goes *Boom.*"

"You're a soldier, right Dad?"

"Ooh-rah and Amen. Yes, my son. Daddy's a soldier."

Dad buys me a lemon-lime Gatorade from the fridge by the cash registers. He is smiling and very far away.

*

I say my father retired from the service because I love him and do not quite know why. I want him protected even though he is dead and feels no goodness or insult, no elation or disenchantment, no pain. I say my father retired because it is true, but I do not say why.

His *forte* was retention: keeping soldiers in once they signed up. For the youngsters, it was selling them hard on the GI Bill—cash for college after you sweat your share for Uncle Sam. And he was sincere in his hopes that "his kids," as he called them, would go to school and get degrees. He was willing to see military service as a pit stop, a means to an end. The old dogs, though, the career guardsmen, were my father's favorite charity.

"If a man," Pop said, "wants to serve his country and he's been doing it for twenty years, who am I to say he has to stop before he gets his pension because he can't run a mile very fast? I follow the rules, but only the ones that make sense." To his credit, Dad tried to follow regulations himself. Once, I came home to find him on the sofa with a dozen White

Castles and three cans of Ultra Slim-Fast. He was watching *FMJ* and it was right at the moment where Hartman threatens the whole platoon:

I will PT you fucks until you vomit through your nostrils and breathe through your asses!

"Your asshole's gonna be sucking buttermilk if you put all that crap in your stomach," I said. "Whiteys and Slim-Fast? Seems counterintuitive."

"Gotta stand on the GI scale tomorrow. Figure I'll orchestrate a nuclear colon blow and come in close enough to the target."

"That may be the most disgusting thing I've ever heard."

"Stand outside the bathroom door in about an hour. It'll get worse. It's the same shit the Army does anyway, just tastier. You ever heard of the green bomb?"
I shook my head.

"Laxative. Weapons-grade. You go to your recruiter and he gives you the old 'Your ass looks like a hundred fifty pounds of chewed bubble gum, Private Pyle.' You start to mope away, but he calls you back. He gives you a horse pill and a magazine and tells you to report for duty in the morning. You take the pill, you shit out things you don't remember eating, and you make weight. After that they feed you a gallon of water, an MRE, and tell you none of this ever happened."

"Sounds like a man speaking from experience, Sarge."

He slurped the last of a Slim-Fast and winked.

No one ever proved that my dad cooked the books at the armory. Nobody ever nailed him for "helping" fat soldiers make weight, or for keeping anyone eligible who was not. But the National Guard took notice and they got Dad's superior, Angie.

"She's a good girl. Wanted out anyway, she's gonna be a school teacher or something. She'll land on her feet," Dad said. The investigation satisfied itself with that, and Pop retired with honor. That night, he watched *Full Metal Jacket* for the thousandth time. As Hartman motherfucked Pyle for failing to climb to the top of an obstacle course ladder wall, Dad's pupils constricted, his jaw set. He wasn't watching anymore but absorbing.

Are you giving up? Hartman screams down at Pyle. Well, are you? Then do it now and get the fuck away from my obstacle course! Now!

Pyle begins his lumbering descent as other Marines—fitter, faster, and in the Drill Instructor's better graces—pass him on either side.

It happened on the screen and inside my father as well; something like a memory stirred as Pop thudded off to bed feeling the wooden rungs of disappointment and otherness under his bare feet. He was beginning to quit and the bedroom door creaked shut behind me and, by the time he closed he eyes, he was starting to die.

*

I was horrified by the sight of Pyle blowing the back of his head out the first time I saw the film.

"You know what that is?" Pop asked.

I was too terrified to speak.
"Exploding tank of ketchup. You could dip fries in that."

*

Gomer Pyle gets a blanket party—four Marines hold a blanket over him, strapping him to the bed. A fifth, Cowboy, gags him. The rest of the platoon files past, beating Pyle in the gut and balls with bars of Ivory wrapped in towels. Dad saw this happen on Christmas, on Father's Day, on the third Thursday of the month when he'd gotten a parking ticket on street cleaning day, on Valentine's Day, on Martin Luther King Day, on Veteran's Day. He saw it every time he watched the film and he never needed a reason or occasion to do that.

*

I have a photo of Pop in Korea with the Air Force during the year he was in the regular Armed Forces. He is wearing an olive drab t-shirt with his gut peeking out the bottom and no pants. He's lying on his side on a cot, laughing at someone outside the frame.

Pyle's beating ends with Joker. As the final Marine to act, he is responsible for administering the blows that the blanket-holders and gag man couldn't. He pounds Pyle's belly once, for himself.

Now, Cowboy whisper-screams. Go on!

One for Cowboy—thump.

One for the right-shoulder man—thump.

One for the left-shoulder man—thump.

Pyle is choking against the gag and thrashing under the blanket. It is powder blue, even in the dark.

One for the left-ankle man—thump.

One for the right-ankle man—thump.

Pyle is screaming "What are you doing," but it sounds like someone trying to gargle and is drowning instead.

Joker rolls onto his bunk directly below Pyle's. Cowboy leans into Pyle's ear and says:

Remember. You had a nightmare, fatshit.

Pyle winces and contorts, he wails and holds his stomach, he bleats like a sheep.

"Why?" he keeps sobbing.

He weeps like my mother at my father's funeral. The final image of the scene is Joker covering his ears.

*

In the photo, Dad looks young and goofy and doughboy-ish. He is on the top bunk.

*

I can't prove Dad watched *Full Metal Jacket* the night before he died. In fact, I can say with certainty that he didn't.

The last time I saw Pop alive was about four in the morning on Friday, June 15, 2007. At nine o'clock that morning, we found his body. Nowhere in the intervening hours could Dad have snuck into the living room for one last screening. But he knew this much: *FMJ* is a film in two parts, which results in it feeling like separate movies altogether. Gomer Pyle is in Act One. His suicide pulls the curtain.

My father had no intention of being in Act Two of my life. He emailed a detailed list of sins and indiscretions to a coworker, which was delivered to me in an envelope after the funeral. Dad's words were different but they read in Pyle's voice. Just before Pyle kills Hartman and himself, Joker tries to stop him. If they're caught, Joker says:

We'll both be in Shit World.

Pyle looks Joker in the face and, in his *tour de force*, screams:

I am!

That's what Pop's final letter said.

How Far Does This Road Go?

I dated a married woman with a dragon tattoo on her back and an orange octopus tattoo on her ass. She was a poet. Together we went to an Oktoberfest disguised as a writer's retreat. It was in the Ozarks of Missouri and, to get there, we had to pass through Texas County. I wore my 10x black felt Stetson for the occasion.

"I like you, Cowboy," she said in the car. Her hand slithered up my leg and into my crotch.

When I took Cowboy for my name, it wasn't about Kubrick at all. Dad had been dead eight years and I was already considering writing about him, but for the moment he was content to stay in the mausoleum of my subconscious. My phobias and proclivities about him got to be momentarily traceless. Not gone, but I didn't know that; they were gone enough. Isn't that what we're all looking to have? A moment where we can plausibly deny the completely fucking obvious? Fact: In my married girlfriend's minivan, thirty-seven miles from the nearest Wal-Mart, it was just me, the vital impulse, my hat, and my new name. Even my lover didn't matter. I was a rodeo for one, complete with clown and catastrophic injury.

*

A movie cowboy rides into an Apache camp and asks the first man he sees:

"Hey Indian, how far does this road go?"

The man is rigid. More stoic than angry? Vice versa? Neither? Both? Who but the man can know what is in his head and heart as he replies:

"Road stay. *You* go."

Dad used to lay his hand flat, palm down, and tell me that was my life.

"You've got all these different paths right now. You haven't had to choose yet."

He'd start closing fingers into a fist, eventually leaving only his pointer extended.

"This one here is the one you commit to. And you have to keep going because you chose—you can't go back. But don't worry about that right now. You're young, enjoy it."

*

I didn't know when I began making this book that I was looking to relieve myself of some of the deep hatred I felt for parts of my father and parts of how his legacy lived in me. I didn't know I was going to thoroughly purge myself of the drive to watch *Full Metal Jacket* again.

I'm sure I will watch it again; this is just a hangover of sorts.

I didn't know anything about where I was going or what I was doing, in truth. There are some memoirists who do— know the arc, the plot, the purpose, the motive of their projects. Some writers can put themselves in front of themselves and have an intrapersonal planning session. This is to say that there are artists, including some I admire a great deal, who probably never get lost in their work.

Such was not the case for me with this book. I started with only the need to breathe about my old man and his movie. It seemed like a straight line. It seemed like following Dad's compass finger. What Pop never really mentioned were the mini forks in the road we choose or the road that chooses us. While other nonfictionists might always understand why we need to make words instead of some alternative, I often wonder, even as this project comes to a close, *Why do I do this to myself?* But I'm on the path and I can't unwalk it. I can't be still, either. The road stays, but I have to go. I don't envy anyone who clearly sees what's ahead. I'd become my father if I saw all that.

*

My friend read this book in an earlier incarnation and had only this to say:

"I wish there were a followable arc of You. I want to see how you've changed."

I wanted to address that and make my friend happy, but at the same time, I was thrown by her calling for a self-consciousness in the present. A majority of this book is reflective, meditative, or in spare instances, predictive. I will try to be present for a moment now and be honest with myself while lying to the reader, as I must.

*

I was born 7 July 1983 in the heat-thick humidity of baseball season. My mother must've gotten pregnant around the time of the previous year's World Series, when the Cardinals beat the Milwaukee Brewers in seven games. I'm a Red Sox fan now, to the chagrin of my childhood friends. The hotel where I work is stumbling distance from Busch Stadium, but the Cardinals lost my heart when I was a teenager and I decided to fall in love with Boston. It would be years and an ill-fated tryst with a red-haired, married woman before I first saw the ocean in Massachusetts, the goldenness of the State House, the armada of ducks in Boston Common, the stalwart kitsch of Cheers, or the sureality of North End. But the Sox were a part of Boston I could tune into and talk about.

We've won three titles together, including 2007, the year my father died. Every time I go to Fenway Park, I cry. Maybe I always will.

*

Boston is also home to some of the oldest cemeteries in America, including the one where Mother Goose is buried. On her headstone is death's head—a skull with some dogged crossbones underneath, almost in the style of the Jolly Roger—and I doubt she had a choice in that. On Dad's headstone there's a Protestant cross. He, too, had no choice in that, but Mom and I did. If you don't know what that looks like, Google it. I had to the first time.

*

I split time between Boston and St. Louis, now. Officially I do it for school, but in truth I only applied to Pine Manor College because it lives in the woods of a suburb of my favorite city. Close friends are always asking for a warning shot before I leave our hometown for good. I demure and say something about real estate prices and Nor'easters, how I survived a Bomb Cyclone once but I wouldn't push my luck, or some other blah-blah of miscellany. I'd be gone tomorrow if I could. I'd go north to South Boston, to a tough Irish enclave where my father's ghost could go to bars with me along with the ghosts of his two youngest brothers. Together, we'd fit right in until I held up my end of the hereditary bargain and lived myself to death by fifty-five. For any evolving I've done, I can't seem to shake the vice that's become a family tradition. My mom's side of the family is guilty in this regard, too, but

I'm old enough now to blame myself for buying into the fatty, fermented, narcotic ethos of being One of Us Guys.

*

I used to steal Winston Lights from my old man's pack after he'd hung his work shirt on the costumer in the front hall. I quit smoking cigarettes ten years ago, except for a month-long relapse after Dad's funeral.

*

Winston is owned by a British company now, headquartered in Bristol; that's just over a hundred miles from the Beckton Gasworks where Kubrick filmed Hue City scenes in *FMJ*. Interestingly enough, I remember the marines all having Marlboros strapped to their helmets. Six months ago, I would've checked.

*

I gave up smoking pot three years ago and for about six years before that. There was a gap year where I would get naked with a sativa-dominant strain and write pantoums in Pig Latin. None of those poems survived the fire, but I'm afraid there might be selfies. Mom knew all about this (well, not that

I was completely naked except for a sombrero, or that I was working in that particular poetic form, but she knew about the ganja) and allowed it because it was easier on my liver than drinking and didn't make me combative. When I started reporting lethargy and feeling like I was growing breasts, she did some research and learned that marijuana counteracts my anti-depressants and stimulates mammary glands in men. I'll tell you that I gave up smoking dope for my mother because it makes me sound stronger and nobler. Let's imagine I did that.

*

I puff cigars daily as of this writing. My favorites are the ACID Kuba Kuba or the Arturo Fuente Hemingway Maduro Perfecto, which go for a couple hundred bucks a box. I've only ever bought two cigars at a time.

*

But that's a miniature catalog of characteristics, nothing of where I am in this immediacy.

*

I'm listening through the basement ceiling as my mother vacuums the living room floor. Pete, our pest control tech, is coming in the morning and we mustn't have a mess while he's waging war with the house centipedes. Thousand-leggers, Mom calls them. We hired Pete after our old neighbor Ian (not Todd, the construction worker who may or may not have walked right past Dad's dead body on his way to a jobsite) called to say he'd seen a rat go into our garage.

"Oh, God, that's awful," I heard Mom say. "Thank you for calling. I'm going to call someone first thing in the morning."

Then, having hung up the phone, she looked at me and said:

"Well isn't that fucking grand. We're going to be The People with a Rat Problem now."

Just like when we'd figured we were going to be The Suicide People or The People Who Had to Move into a Rental Because the Provider Left Them. Just like a lot of Peoples we have mercifully yet to become. But the rat was real, and we hired Pete to come kill him, which he did.

There's a part in *The Short-Timers* where two platoons with rage and energy to spare have a rat-stomping contest; they light a fire in their hooches to frighten the hell out of the rats and make them scatter, then they stomp and bayonet as many as they can. Winner gets bragging rights.

I almost didn't put that in because I'm not sure I care. Seeing it now, I'm still not sure. I do remember being horrified, especially when one of the marines takes a bite of one of the roasted rats.

Mom's vacuum sounds like a low-flying drone doing recon. Actually, it sounds like what it is.

*

James Kirby invented the first American domestic vacuum in 1906, long after the invention of rats but well before we'd ever heard of drones. Mom and I exist in the limbo between histories, as always. I'm not even mad.

*

I'm not always exactly where I am. The vacuum is a memory from hours ago.

*

I'm waiting for a beer to be poured by a heavyset bartender who doesn't flirt with me just for tips. I'm thinking about mute consonants, liquid consonants, and the definition of pillory. (Attack or ridicule publicly, unless referring to a pillory beach, which I'm not.) But mostly I'm thinking about bucking the conventions of memoir on accident and how it registers as neither a trophy nor a goddamn shame. In *Living Autobiographically,* Paul John Eakin rightly points to the enormous amount of fiction we not only tolerate but have come to expect in our memoirs—we know all about the con-artistry of memory and the inescapable impulse to fudge things for the sake of being more interesting. I know I should give you more of what I realized and when—give you little flashbangs of reflection or epiphany. But Charles Baxter tells us (speaking of fiction) that epiphany is overrated. If we're bullshitting ourselves and one another, even when we tell the truest stories we own, why not shake the style tree and see what fruit falls down?

*

Listen: I grew up in a house full of poles. There was God and the devil; right and wrong; sin and righteousness. There was Mom the Nurturer and Dad the Disciplinarian. There was good honest labor, which my father claimed to do, and there was shysterism, which described anyone who made more than ten thousand dollars per year more than Dad did.

I remember going into the front hall while my father unburdened himself of his boots.

"Good evening, my child," he said.

I answered by throwing my young body at his aging one. It wasn't a hug, but an ambush.

"What's wrong with you?" Pop asked.

"Nothing. I'm just depressed."

"Bullshit. What's really wrong?"

"That is what's really wrong."

"Goddamn it boy, I get enough of this shit from my wife. I get the blues sometimes, too. There's nothing wrong with that. But it's not the same as being mentally whatever-she-calls-it."

"Ill, Dad. Mentally ill."

"I fucking know what she says, Andrew. Don't you start now too."

There was occasional sadness and craziness. That's how I was raised. There were borders of extremes while the grey area was off limits—it was some sea in which we'd all drown if we dared dip a metaphorical toe. My old man wouldn't talk about his feelings. There was only what he saw and what he treasured, like Mary did with the gifts of the wise men.

*

Listen: all my epiphanies came on the heels of disaster. I only realize things after I've died a bit inside. Don't ask me for that, friend. I'm begging you.

*

My barkeep's name is Cynthia and she pours Guinness straight down in one sitting instead of the Dublin three-step. Nobody else here notices, so I don't say anything. It's not as important as telling you the bar top is linoleum and reminds me of the kitchen floor I grew up with. Booze and its delivery aren't as important as telling you that I spend every second praying I don't become my father. I'm a foul-mouth adulterer, and I have authority resentment problems. I'm starting to really need that drink, Cynthia. Even counting the number of Garth Brooks songs that play in a row on the jukebox isn't soothing anymore.

I grew up almost exclusively on country music and had to ask my dad's permission to try out Rock and Roll. He was afraid the lyrics of bands like Guns 'N Roses would be a bad influence, push me in the wrong direction. I had Kenny Rogers and George Strait because they were wholesome. But at the same time I had the gruesome spectacle of *Full Metal Jacket* because it was honest. More honest than Dad was, anyhow, and more worldly. I wonder—no, fuck that—I *know* that my father was as every bit as jealous of the perceived homegrown goodness of country ballads as he was of the silver-screen masculinity of grunts in *FMJ*.

I feast on irony, too. I will flay the old man for it but indulge myself at the same moment. I'm no better than him. No worse, either.

*

I got into a wonderful debate in a bar just like the one where I waited for Cynthia to pour my Guinness wrong. A guy came in drunk and told me the oldest autobiography in the world was the Bible because God wrote all of it, just with someone else's hands. I asked the guy if it didn't matter that a big-ass chunk of the Bible isn't about God at all, but about who begat whom and how many cubits one Jacobite or another's field was. Most of the Old Testament makes you wonder *Why am I reading this?*

What does this guy say to all this? Fucked if I remember.

*

Listen: I'm not exhausted enough to tell you how this ends, and I'm not smart enough either. See, I'm not God, but I still believe in Her. She'll write another chapter, however many verses long, and whatever I picked out for the ending—my own little paper apocalypse—won't mean shit. Maybe She'll inspire a whole other Bible. Where will I be then if I'm not still here? Do we get kicked out of the heaven we went to by mistake? Does hell turn out to be listening to Johnny Wright while watching combat veterans self-destruct, and Stanley Kubrick is the devil?

We're winding out into the weird. The irrelevant. Come back with me to the simplest idea: I can't tell you *this* is over. The book ends, but the story doesn't. In this way, my life really is like *Full Metal Jacket.*

FMJ ends with a column of Marines marching to the mismatched cadence of the Mickey Mouse Club anthem. They are giddy, maybe. Relieved. Terrified. Their singing and their walking give us nothing but sensory data: they sound and look alive. For now.

I'm still hanging around, working at a hotel, drinking beer, moving sentences around, watching or waiting to watch baseball, petting every dog I see. I am not a moving epiphany, don't you see? I don't plan on having kids, because I don't want to fuck them up the way my old man fucked up me; if that changes, if I decide to have (or end up having) children, that'll be epiphanic. If I put a gun in my mouth and become life imitating life and resulting in death, that'll be epiphanic.

There's nothing earthshaking about simply being alive, until you understand that you have the choice not to be. My father's suicide freed me to either live or die. Either one is, in some form, a choice, a decision. Today I decided to live. I can't promise you anything about tomorrow or ten weeks from now.

*

Here's your epiphany:

M-I-C, K-E-Y, M-O-U-S-E.

Mickey Mouse.

Mickey Mouse.

DANCING THROUGH THE TWITTERVERSE

Nobody wants to talk to me. I once wrote a letter to the mayor of a small Indiana town in response to his statement inferring his constituents were too good to commit suicide. He responded with a terse denial, followed by unending silence. I tried sending an email to Charles Manson's prison inbox under the pretenses of interviewing him about his newfound humanitarian façade; no reply, no return to sender, not a goddamn thing. It shouldn't surprise me too much that Vincent D'Onofrio hasn't tweeted back at me yet. What's curious is his prolific interactions with his other Twitter followers.

Vincent D'Onofrio @vincentdonofrio

This is a joke tweet right? It's very funny. If
it's not a joke, you should start reading both
left&right newspapers&online journalists.
Read both get ur facts correct . . .
find the TRUTH.

Greg @Greg'sTwitterHandle

You realize wut Donald Trump has done with a
hostile congress and a year's time? Makes you
reconsider all the propaganda you believed
about Killary.

This content is emblematic of a larger theme in Vince's
feed: he has an active dislike for POTUS Trump.

Vincent D'Onofrio @vincentdonofrio

Our Prez. Oh Boy.

[Large black and white photo of POTUS looking
frumpy. He is slouching and wearing an unstructured white
ballcap that hasn't been adjusted to fit. He's also wearing an
unzipped
    rain slicker. He looks like a confused child on his first
camping
    trip with the Boy Scouts. Minus any innocence or
sympathetic
    qualities, of course. The hat is emblazoned with the
letters
    USA.]

My reply is one of nearly fifty, all the same ilk.

Andy Smart @AndyMakesWords (replying to @vincentdonofrio)

That better be an acronym for Unsupervised Saprophyte Asshole. Otherwise he needs to take it off. #resist45

At present, Vince hasn't responded. But he might. I'm losing hope, but there's still a chance, because Vince is alive and he has the prerogative to interact with me or not; in this, he is unlike the others to whom I've reached out. The mayor of that quaint Indiana township has closed his mind to me; Charles Manson is dead; my father, too, to whom I've written more than once, is gone. The ache of Vince's refusal to take a moment and chat is a special kind thereof—the nagging, annoying, festering kind.

My attempts at seducing Vince into dialogue began in 2015. It was my first tweet, I believe, and read something like this:

Andy Smart @WhateverHandleIUsed

@vincentdonofrio I'm writing my master's thesis about Full Metal Jacket. Talk to me? Please?

All I knew was that tweets were supposed to be pithy. Three people "liked" the tweet, but no one replied. Two years later, after a full-on hiatus from Twitter, I am writing the thesis to which I alluded the first time. I began the campaign to converse with Vince all over in hopes of a better result.

Andy Smart @AndyMakesWords

@vincentdonofrio I'm writing my Master's thesis about Full Metal Jacket. Any chance you'd take a few questions?

Mean the world to me.

Lisa "liked" this tweet because I asked her to. She said something about amplifying my reach. I owned up to not knowing what that meant. But Vince remained silent. Silent towards me, that is.

The same day his feed was alive with questions about his character on *Daredevil*, his stance on net-neutrality, and petitions for virtual hugs.

Nancy @Nancy'sTwitterHandle

@vincentdonofrio My only Christmas wish is one more Twitter hug from you. ::hugs::

Melody @Melody'sTwitterHandle

@vincentdonofrio My mother would've been 90 years old today. She died of cancer and I miss her every Christmas.

Can I have a hug?

Dan @Dan'sTwitterHandle

@vincentdonofrio I graduated from film school today! So glad

I get to share my day with you. Big fan of you, buddy!

Vince's army of tweeting fans is huge and vocal. I watched the feed anxiously, waiting for him to take to the keys and reply to a couple of them.

I began counting the tweets Vince answered. And then I gave up counting.

Vincent D'Onofrio @vincentdonofrio (replying to Melody/Dan/Nancy/Name/Name/Place/Name)

Thanks for following, I'm proud of you!! Big Hug!

(or)

Hugs. That's a tough one.

(or)

Happy Holidays friend. Hug.

(or)

I'm not sure where you get your political info. You obviously

need a hug.

(or)

[Thoughtful, germane, occasionally grammatically shoddy response, usually sans emojis.]

(or)

Vincent D'Onofrio @vincentdonofrio (replying to @AndyMakesWords)

[Nothing.]

I was no more dejected than I was pissed off; this is to say I was very much both. But, as the hard-headed son of a stubborn Scots-Irishman, I took Vince's quietude as a challenge. Hello cape, I am raging bull. If Vince would only interact with the bleeding, the boorish, or the jubilant, I would call up a picador of personal tragedy and let it wound me anew; then I'd tweet my torn flesh and Vince would be hooked. I had no momentous occasion to celebrate and no debate to enter into. I'd have to use my insides.

Andy Smart @AndyMakesWords

@vincentdonofrio My dad shot himself just like Gomer Pyle in

Full Metal Jacket. He was a lot like him. Is there any Leonard

Lawrence that you carry around with you?

There it was. I had done what I swore not to, ever: I'd traded on my father's suicide. I'd used the trauma of truth for presumptive gain. I was a whore on the internet.

Why, precisely, did Vince's commentary on *Full Metal Jacket*, or on my old man's death, or on what film can (and should) do in POTUS Trump's America, or on whether it's pissing in the wind to tweet at famous people matter to me? Why'd it matter enough to auction off my honor with the obvious risk that nobody would bid on it?

A: I've internalized the character of Gomer Pyle as my father as much as my father did.

B: I am blind and dumb when the almighty Writing is involved and I'll do anything for it, accordingly.

C: Whoredom is a maligned, but not evil, occupation.

D: All of the above, plus some more.

This is not a teacher's copy; there are no answers here.

A whore with no clients is still a whore, but the judgment is less harsh from the outside. Vince didn't answer the tweet about my father's blown-off head. He didn't give me a hug or a pat on the head or an inspirational quote from the bible. Not a meme. He gave me blankness.

In the days of dial-up internet, he would've given me a busy signal.

I thought about it. I bitched about it. I decided it was probably a matter of subject—Vince didn't want to talk about *FMJ*. It was his start, the jumping-off point of a career; to go back there is remedial success. Besides, from everything I'd read about Kubrick, he was a taskmaster for the ages, settling only for a product featuring its cast on their most ragged of edges. I wanted to tweet Vince and ask him if playing Gomer Pyle was worth it. I imagined him tweeting back that he wasn't sure.

I stalked his feed again, mining for reasons he'd ignored me and looking for different inroads into the social component of his social media.

One of the starkest scenes in *Full Metal Jacket* doesn't involve Gomer Pyle at all. Instead, Joker and Rafterman are standing over a mass grave. The bodies are covered in lime. In my real-time homage to the film, there is a shot of me sitting in front of a monitor full of tweets from Vince regarding *FMJ*. Kubrick makes Joker tell us: The dead only know that being alive is better. These tweets know more than they are telling, but they are telling a thing nonetheless. It is better to know this much.

Vincent D'Onofrio @vincentdonofrio (replying to @Barbara'sTwitterHandle)
We knew each other from auditions and classes
in NYC.

Barbara @Barbara'sTwitterHandle

@vincentdonofrio IIRC, it was Matthew Modine who
suggested you for the role in FMJ, am I right? How
did you know each other in the first place?

Vincent D'Onofrio @vincentdonofrio (replying to User @User'sTwitterHandle)

Every extra in FMJ was either Irish, Scottish, or
British w/1 American. I hung out with a few of the
English lads&the american. We had laughs& many
hours of fun just talking nonsense. I was able 2get2
know them well. I think about those guys often. I wish
them well. They were very kind2me.

User @User'sTwitterHandle

@ vincentdonofrio What are your enduring memories of

. . . filming 'Full Metal Jacket'?

Then there are bedfellow question and answer exchanges
about acting at large. This one, especially, struck a jealous
chord in me:

Vincent D'Onofrio @vincentdonofrio (replying to
Bugsy @Bugsy'sTwitterHandle)

Yes, exactly. Not that you don't try and take it all
the way. You do.
It is rare when you would ever have2push yourself
2the edge becuz in life we rarely do if ever. But yes
when the director says cut you learn2appreciate
what you just succeeded in rather than dwelling
on it.
Its a trip.

Bugsy @Bugsy'sTwitterHandle

@vincentdonofrio So is there a balance sought
between the uncharted territory of a unique
character and your own emotional equilibrium
and stamina?

The artist welcomes the edge but divorces himself from the plunge off the cliff. Are there clichés embedded in this knowing? I learn, but I learn at a slant. What is clear is that Vince is a craftsman and a survivor. Is he risen above the realm of me and my inquiring mind?

Look, Andrew, look. How many of these tweets are responses to responses to responses? You are joining a conversation about conversations, son. Thus spoke the voice of my father as imagined by me and influenced by everyone.

It's true. I'd have to wade through the muck of a million tweets to see if Vince has already answered my questions. But they were not mine, though they look the same. They did not come from the wanting places in my belly, the nightmarish needfulness of a fatherless son. *This* fatherless son.

There must be a way to connect. Maybe a banality, like the huggers use:

Andy Smart @AndyMakesWords

@vincentdonofrio Which is harder for you personally: working on something that isn't fulfilling or not working at all?

It's an inquiry bland enough that even I'm not interested in the answer. This is a pride battle now, a shameless bid to get a nod. When I first conceived this piece, it was meant to be my *tour de force*: A Conversation with Vincent D'Onofrio. Ego: that's what's killing me about Vince and his selective silences. I thought my experiences and my infinite charm were the turnkey into unprecedented access to Vince's memories, his philosophies and regrets, the closet in which remains the fatigues he wore as Gomer Pyle. But they're not. I am a fan, or more appropriately, a groupie. I confess: when the Twittersphere throws Vince a ticker-tape parade because one of the characters he plays at present has done something grand, I'm lost. I'm not like the others, the ones who get hugs and pseudo-interviews.

I want to use Vince for Gomer, like my father did before me, and Vince isn't having it. Do I blame him? No more than I blame *Full Metal Jacket* for being what it is. I am kicking a hornet's nest full of dead drones and I'm getting back the echoes of futility. Pvt. Pyle has definitely been born again, hard.

*

What is a thwarted internet troll to do? Delight in some of what proves to me that Vince is not my old man:

Vincent D'Onofrio @vincentdonofrio (replying to: Trumpers @MyGodThey'reEverywhere)

I'm a Dem and consider this a brag. Yes I'm for
equal rights and civil liberties for all. For all in
the world. I'm a Democratic and a snowflake
liberal waving my flag. My American flag. Same
flag you have.

Trumpers @MyGodThey'reEverywhere

@vincentdonofrio I wouldn't run around bragging about being a Democrat. That's not something you brag about.

Two things here make the wheels fall off: Democrat and snowflake. Dad would've loved Trae Crowder (YouTube's Liberal Redneck) but would've never had the chutzpah to call himself a crystallized fluff of winter precipitation. His bravado wouldn't have allowed it. And to say Pop was a Democrat is stretching the truth ever-so-slightly. He was, until his dying day, what he called an Independent. Not like the occasionally-almost-relevant Third-Party Candidates; truly, he wanted everybody listed, from all parties, on one ballot to so he could decide *in situ*. Besides, as he put it:

"Ain't anybody else's fuckin' business who I'm voting for. That's what makes this country great: I can vote for the best candidate and everybody else can be fuckin' stupid."

It makes me wonder: am I really nipping at Vince's heels because I want to talk to my dad? And, inevitably, I'm coming up disappointed? Even if I sat Vince down over brunch somewhere in Brooklyn, it wouldn't be the earthshaking event I dreamt it up to be. It'd be two guys talking. Probably very briefly. What I actually want is to chirp at my father in the afterlife via some postmortem media platform:

Andy Smart @AndyMakesWords

@SgtDad Remember the scene in FMJ where Pyle gets busted for the jelly doughnut in his footlocker? They just built a Dunkin right by Mom's gynecologist.
See what you're missing?
(or)

Andy Smart @AndyMakesWords

@SgtDad Alabama told Roy Moore to kick rocks! How's that for Roll Tide? #notbadforpoorwhitetrash

(or)

Andy Smart @AndyMakesWords

@SgtDad Love you, Pop.

That's what I want. If the old man were here, I can safely guarantee he'd be on Twitter. His handle would probably be something like his Match.com screen name, or maybe he would've gone with Sergeant Dad. It's an irrelevant piece of convolution: feeling some kind of nostalgia for an impossible future.

Maybe I'll start a feed in Dad's honor, see if Vince will talk to him. Now I sound like a man possessed.

There was one tweet from Vincent D'Onofrio that chilled me where the rest had either been warm and fuzzy or unaffecting. Someone asked him if there was any role he couldn't master; if there was any character he couldn't become. Anything he couldn't "knock out of the park."

Vincent D'Onofrio @vincentdonofrio

I'll die trying.

I believe he almost did—die trying to inhabit, portray, execute, and escape Gomer Pyle—and I think he is afraid. It's a bit like the warning that used to come on the side mirrors of cars:

"Objects in Mirror Are Closer Than They Appear."

You're not Leonard Lawrence, Vince. You're not Jeff Smart, or my buddy either. You're a left-leaning actor with a daughter who lives in California and is a hell of a dancer; I checked out the video you tweeted earlier this week. You've been on *Law and Order*, too, which is pretty kickass. You live your life in manageable strides away from wherever you just were.

Pick 'em up and set 'em down.

Tweet, retweet, like, comment, favorite. Log out.

No, It Isn't: An Academic Investigation

*

The popular, if not prevailing, view of Stanley Kubrick's *Full Metal Jacket* is that it's an antiwar picture. The film is referred to in this nomenclature specifically in Gene D. Phillips and Rodney Hill's 2002 book *Great Filmmakers The Encyclopedia of Stanley Kubrick From Day of the Fight to Eyes Wide Shut*. Phillips and Hill, among other critics, make the seemingly inevitable conclusion that Kubrick's film—a violently comedic 116 minutes of cruelty, irony, and contradiction—takes a stance against the very war Kubrick selected for his subject, or perhaps armed conflict in general.

While this is handy, and certainly logical, it's not quite true. Nothing about Kubrickian cinema is that easily pigeonholed. To say *FMJ* is anti-war would be tantamount to calling *A Clockwork Orange* anti-teenager. While I can claim no comprehensive expertise in the field of cinematography or film criticism, I have watched *Full Metal Jacket* almost as obsessively as my father did. I've read about it, talked about it, dreamt about it, and I can't subscribe to the ideology that

Kubrick was making an antiwar statement with this movie. This essay will explore three sources to which I turn to build my case: the film itself, the books on which the film is based (Gustav Hasford's *The Short-Timers* and Michael Herr's *Dispatches)*, and Michael Herr's own account of working with Kubrick on the film.

Before I begin, however, I want to acknowledge the merits of the antiwar definition of *Full Metal Jacket*. As viewers, we do not (if I may universalize a bit) take pleasure in seeing the beatings and berating handed down at Parris Island. We don't want Gomer Pyle to be bullied into madness and suicide. We don't thrill to, enjoy, or even understand Crazy Earl's exploitation of a dead Vietnamese corpse. As an audience, we are glad to be in our seats instead of "in the shit" with the grunts. *Full Metal Jacket* produces, in many people including myself, strong antiwar sentiments. These reactions, however, cannot be projected onto the film; the art is a product, our response is our own, apart from the art we're responding to. I will show, in time, that art is precisely what Stanley Kubrick intended *Full Metal Jacket* to be. Art which can be dissected and construed in myriad ways completely irrelevant to the original intent: to make a good movie.

*

Full Metal Jacket begins with a song. Johnny Wright croons his saccharine tune "Hello, Vietnam" while the recruits receive their GI buzz cuts. In *Listening to Stanley Kubrick*, Dr.

Christine Gengaro offers this observation: Kubrick deliberately leaves out the sound of the clippers. Wright's lyrics, then, are the first voice we hear. If we examine said lyrics, a clear strategy emerges on Kubrick's part: recall the ethos of Vietnam-era America and use it to frame the action to come. It's the first of many ironies; this one happens to be some sweetness in the strychnine.

"Kiss me goodbye and write me while I'm gone," Wright intones. It hearkens back to numerous other war films, making us imagine a soldier in the field rereading the same creased and tattered letter from his gal over and over. It's a warm image on its face. But Wright goes on, only a few lines later, to prophesy: "I don't believe that war will ever end / There's fighting that will break us up again." And here we have it. A nod to the permanence of war—the interminable human engagement in its own destruction. Neither Wright nor Kubrick makes any over gestures to protest this perpetual warfare, either.

In fact, Wright's lyrics take a turn for, ostensibly, the pro-military in the closing stanzas of "Hello, Vietnam": "We must stop communism in that land / or freedom will start slipping through our hands"; "I hope and pray someday the world will learn / that fires we don't put out will bigger burn."

Wright—and Kubrick by extension—isn't pointing to war as a negative, unless we put undue stress on the romantic breakup, which serves as a subtext to Wright's track. What Kubrick achieves here is a resurrection of American thinking at the outset of this particular police action. (Or, for the hippies and conscientious objectors, it reminds them of what they'd opposed even then.) It's emotive, yes. But it's not didactic.

Kubrick maintains his pop culture submersion technique throughout *Full Metal Jacket*. As Dr. Gengaro notes:

"*Full Metal Jacket* was Kubrick's first film in a decade to eschew classical or art music as part of the score. As Kubrick discovered in *Dr. Strangelove*, popular music can be very powerful in the . . . ways it creates meaning for the viewer.

At the time of the film's release, many viewers of *Full Metal Jacket* were old enough to remember both the war and the music Kubrick chose for his soundtrack" (60).

The inclusion of hits like "These Boots Were Made for Walking," "Wooly Bully," and the outro, "Paint it Black" are all chosen for their emotive qualities and historical appropriateness. While there couldn't have been much doubt in Kubrick's mind that there would be a strong evocation of antiwar sentiment, I maintain that this evocation is a byproduct of Kubrick's overarching commitment to making an honest, cinematically masterful, and historically accurate film.

Even my estimation of Kubrick's aim is incomplete and quite possibly overcomplicated. According to Michael Herr's biography of Kubrick, the director saw *Full Metal Jacket* as "another Who Do You Root For Movie" (*Kubrick*, 37). His basic concern with this film, as Herr and others assert, is the dual nature of humanity; Kubrick set out to make a film depicting the dichotomous, yet simultaneous, existence of compassion and violence, of good and evil. Phillips and Hill note that: "Asked about the deeper implications of the picture,

Kubrick usually replied that the film is built around the concept of . . . altruism and cooperation on the one hand, aggression and xenophobia on the other" (128).

The film itself gives us explicit grounding in Kubrick's philosophy; Matthew Modine's character, Private Joker, is caught wearing a peace button on his helmet, upon which Joker has also written Born To Kill. A hardboiled Colonel approaches Joker and asks him if the combo is some kind of joke.

I was commenting on man and his duality duality Sir, Joker replies.

What follows is more veiled autobiography. The colonel asks Joker if he loves America.

Yes, Sir!

Kubrick, too, loved America, despite a long and self-imposed exile in England. According to Michael Herr, "America was all [Kubrick] ever talked about. It was always on his mind, and in his blood" (46). But this patriotism was not rosy enough to dissuade the director from unpretentious realism in some of his work, most notably *Full Metal Jacket*. "Stanley had views on everything, but I wouldn't exactly call them political," Herr writes (12). Kubrick was a moderate— hopeful but jaded; proud but not a jingo; "his views on democracy were those of most people I know" (12).

While he may have had objections to the American system of government, or at least qualms with it, there is one thing about Kubrick that is well documented; he was a capitalist. On its surface this fact seems irrelevant, but consider this; how likely is a filmmaker who is both profit-minded and notoriously cheap to make a movie based around a political ideal, as opposed to focusing on marketability? Kubrick wouldn't gamble on a statement picture; enough people with strong pro-military attitudes wouldn't see what they thought of as an antiwar flick.

Besides the commercially reckless nature of stance-taking, Kubrick's own political conviction was more that America would be its best under "a benign despot" who could salvage the remains of a dwindling "liberal humanism" (12). Liberal humanism is admittedly a slippery subject; my attempts to research it were truncated by the migraines reading about it induced. The main thrust of this theory, however, is that mankind is the focal point of everything— man as an agent of his own destiny or situation. It's a theoretical approach, which is based heavily on freedom (and this is where the convolutedness comes barreling through: what does it mean to be free? why are there inequities in freedom across genders and cultures? how is man free if he's governed by reason?).

Therefore, bearing in mind that Kubrick already viewed *Full Metal Jacket* as a "Who Do You Root For Movie," we must view the film through a thickly layered lens. Liberal humanism does not (as far as I've been able to ascertain) address violence or warfare explicitly. However, it grants man the agency to fight for his convictions, or to fight for any reason at all. Being, as man is, possessed of the dual nature between peace and violence, he is now authorized to exercise his judgment. Once in the throes of a fight like Vietnam the choice, as audiences see, makes itself: kill or be killed.

Do we root against the presumptive protagonists because the gratuitous violence of *Full Metal Jacket* is distasteful? I don't.

*

One of the most prevalent cases made for *Full Metal Jacket*'s status as antiwar is how affected some of the characters are by the violence of the film. In many instances, the conversation goes no further than the opening act on Parris Island. Obviously, Gomer Pyle's transformation from oafish tub of lard into deranged, suicidal, super-Marine is disturbing; if it weren't for Vietnam, Leonard Lawrence (Pyle's given name) wouldn't be in the Marine Corps to begin with. Therefore, isn't the spectacle of Pyle's suffering and death an indictment against war? Not exactly.

In her essay collection, *The Art of Cruelty*, Maggie Nelson speaks to "theatre of cruelty," a term coined by Antonin Artaud and expounded upon—in various degrees of directness and completeness—by others. Artaud's cruelty was what "cements matter together . . . molds the features of the created world" ("Theatres of Cruelty," 18). In Artaud's shadow, if not in his footsteps, came Italian Futurism, championed by F.T. Marinetti. In "The Founding and Manifesto of Futurism," Marinetti declares:

"Art can be nothing but violence, cruelty, and injustice' and promises 'to glorify war—the world's only hygiene' along with 'militarism . . . and scorn for woman" (19).

Beyond the gore mongering, this type of art had a lofty, careless aim; it collapses the distance between the artist, the art, and the audience. Nelson writes:

"Any time an audience remains intact enough to shuffle out murmuring *how powerful* before deciding where to have their pie and Schnapps, Artaud's dream of 'crushing and hypnotizing the spectator,' perhaps to the point of no return, has died" (18).

To crush and hypnotize the audience, perhaps to the point of no return. That's what *Full Metal Jacket* aims to do, and it does. I've seen it happen.

*

It's a matter of public record by this point: My father loved *Full Metal Jacket*. He pointed to it as a prime example of how not only war, but also the military and maybe even manhood are at large. His relationship with the film blossomed from love into obsession, and from obsession into imitation. From imitation, it graduated to participation, which is precisely what futurist art strives for. Jacques Ranciere (as quoted by Maggie Nelson) states: "Spectatorship is a bad thing . . . looking is deemed the opposite of acting" ("Theatres of Cruelty," 24). If my father hadn't picked up his pistol on June 15, 2007 and shot himself in the head, just as his favorite cinematic counterpart Gomer Pyle does, *Full Metal Jacket* would be a futuristic failure. The capacity of the film to subsume my old man this completely makes it exemplary of what Artaud, Marinetti, and others sought to do.

Let us return to Parris Island and the plight of Gomer Pyle on the screen but let us also take the futurists and the theatres of cruelty along. It is true that Pyle's treatment is cruel. Though Hartman aims to mold him into a field marine, motivation does not trump results. The rest of the platoon begins as spectators of a sort. While they, too, are abused physically and emotionally, they adapt while Pyle languishes in his perpetual incompetence. The volta for the platoon, some of whom like Joker, have even tried to aid Pyle, comes in the jelly doughnut scene.

Each recruit stands atop his footlocker. Each man is in his boxers and a plain white t-shirt, barefoot and with his hands palms-down in front of him. Hartman walks the aisle and barks commands like Clip your fingernails, Pop your blister, and so on. We, the viewers, see it coming; Pyle will naturally do something wrong here. He must. When Hartman discovers Pyle has left his footlocker unlocked, the punishment is swift and severe: Pyle's belongings are chucked across the squad bay, clattering across the deck. And there, in the bottom of Pyle's footlocker, is an embezzled jelly doughnut.

The fuck have you got there? Hartman demands.

What follows is more of the expected cruelty: Hartman hurls insults while Pyle stands like a somehow-wounded statue. Then, however, Hartman subverts the expected action.

Privat Pyle, Hartman informs his ever-hardening grunts, has ruined not only his honor but the whole platoon's. This constitutes a failure of morale. Clearly the other recruits haven't brought Private Pyle into the fold by motivating him to get his shit together. From this point forward, then, Pyle's fuck ups are the platoon's fuck ups and they will all pay for them. Everybody *except* Private Pyle.

The scene closes with Pyle munching his doughnut while the rest of the recruits do pushups.

Thus begins the collapse of one type of distance between watching and acting. For a while, the recruits suffer their increased workload when Pyle makes a mistake. But their patience has limits. Ultimately, the other marines give Private Pyle a blanket party: four men hold Pyle down under a blanket while a fifth gags him; the rest of the recruits file past and pummel him with bar soap rolled in towels. Finally, Joker strikes Pyle not only for himself, but for those who couldn't because they were restraining their victim.

Cowboy, Joker, and the others are now participants as opposed to spectators, which changes their relationship with the audience. Consciously or otherwise, *Full Metal Jacket* takes a prototypically futurist tack.

As for Pyle's suicide, the most traumatic, visceral moment in the film, this, too, is a nod to both futurism and Kubrick's liberal humanism. As Maggie Nelson asks, in "Theatres of Cruelty": "Whether an act of so-called violence must always be characterized or accompanied by cruelty . . . [such as] some instances of suicide" (21). Pyle is seen, finally, as self-possessed. He not only exercises his freedom to take his own life (and act that Schopenhauer would applaud) but also to kill Hartman and spare Joker. Pyle's death is attended by a sort of bifold mercy; he ends his own suffering and does not lash out against the closest thing he's had to a friend. Even in the calamitous cruelty of Parris Island, Pyle's duality is intact. War—or the preparation for and specter thereof—have not destroyed it. Gomer Pyle's suicide is not antiwar, but pro-human. It's a weird, Kubrickian hope.

*

Full Metal Jacket is based on two books: Gustav Hasford's novel *The Short-Timers* and Michael Herr's war correspondence collection, *Dispatches*. Both of these books contain considerably more antiwar-esque elements than the film they inspired.

In *The Short-Timers*, Hasford characterizes the violence enacted upon the recruits as more of a sport than any kind of attempt at instruction. Gunny Gerheim, the Drill Instructor in the novel, is portrayed as a short, stout bully who likes to take recruits into the shower—out of view of the others—where they will "fall down" and have some unsurprising bruises as a result.

The narrator, too, is an unexpected voice if one is reading the book after seeing the film, like I did. Hasford's narrator is sort of like the Joker we know from Kubrick, but considerably more intensely Marine-ish. Hasford's narrator becomes wildly gung-ho and bloodlusty—to the point that he is reassigned to a unit of grunts, where our enduring image of him is that of a hardcore killer. Hasford's narrator actually executes Cowboy in a mercy killing; unlike Kubrickian mercy (after witnessing Pyle's suicide, Joker goes on to mercy kill a Vietnamese sniper just before the film's end), however, Hasford's narrator is accompanied by an exchange of mutual vitriol between shooter and target.

We could apply the futurist litmus test to *The Short-Timers,* but I think it would fail. Hasford's perspective—a first person, semi-omniscient narrator—feels more like a statement than Kubrick's film. Also, given that Gustav Hasford served in Vietnam, the likelihood that his (thinly veiled) autobiographical fiction is imbued with some personal opinion about the war is quite high. Kubrick's knowledge and perception of the war were the product of auto-didactic fascination and a lot of other war films.

Michael Herr's *Dispatches* is also considerably more antiwar than *Full Metal Jacket,* though its futurist compliance is obvious: it's a book about a man going from writing and thinking about war, to writing, thinking, and being directly imperiled by said war. Herr's antiwar statements, however, are more politically specific. He points to the overarching censorship of war journalism, as Kubrick includes in the film.

Shortly after the second act of *FMJ* opens, Joker is harassed by Lockhart for not including any kills in his coverage of a recent firefight:

We run two storylines here, Lockhart says. The first one is heartwarming bullshit and the second one is how we're kicking Charlie's ass.

He goes on to say that while some people might want readers in the U.S. to feel bad about the war, that's not what battle correspondents do. They keep up morale and they take headshots at awards ceremonies.

Herr includes a lot of these types of anecdotes in the "Illumination Rounds" and "Colleagues" sections of *Dispatches*. Vietnam revolutionized the way war was delivered to home audiences. For the first time, TV wouldn't allow for some of the whitewashing of wartime truths. Instead, it sometimes encouraged American military brass to dial up offensives when they knew correspondents were around; give the folks at home a good show, let them know that—as Kubrick calls it in *Full Metal Jacket*—Mother Green and Her Killing Machine are still the baddest of the bad. Thinking of it now, perhaps Herr's narrative isn't as much antiwar as anti-propaganda. Herr begs the question then, which I'll ask now: what is different between the two?

Kubrick, too, acknowledges the role of bravado and groupthink in fighting. As Pratap Rughani notes in his essay "Kubrick's Lens: Dispatches from the Edge," the contrasting scenes in *Full Metal Jacket*, where the Lusthog squad is filmed *en masse* versus individually, showcase the radical shift in collective versus individual attitude. "In single interviews," Rughani notes, "squad members sound more like individuals . . . carrying their own questions" (*Kubrick: New Perspectives*, 322).

This insight, which Rughani refers to as "the camera as X-ray machine," is fascinating, but doesn't constitute an antiwar jab. It is, quite simply, Kubrickian. In his biography of Stanley Kubrick, Michael Herr points to the director's fascination with "clinical exactness" alongside "abiding irreality" (27) as well as "why . . . all war movies look . . . phony." Kubrick doesn't express an opinion about his subject here; he simply presents it with the degree of engineered authenticity he deems best and allows audience agency to assign meaning or relevance to any or all the film's elements.

*

We've come a long way. My basic thesis is that *Full Metal Jacket* is not an antiwar film, despite eliciting antiwar reactions from many viewers and being referred to as such by critics. I've attempted to illustrate the roles of Kubrick's personality (his fascination with realism and the complexity of human nature, as well as making a good film), the source materials he worked from (which, according to Michael Herr, were always a thing Kubrick revered, no matter what the project at hand happened to be; interestingly, for almost all of Kubrick's films, there is documentable source matter), and futurist film critique have on understanding *Full Metal Jacket*.

I've also tried to demonstrate how acquaintances like Michael Herr describe Kubrick's attitudes toward film in general, and *Full Metal Jacket* specifically. When Kubrick first approached Herr, for instance, he simply said he wanted to make a war movie but wasn't sure about which war.

I've tried to relive the memories of watching my old man watch this movie. I've collapsed the distance again. I used to watch him watch; then I watched with him; now, according to my metaphysics, he watches me watch *Full Metal Jacket*.

Maybe I've spread myself too thin here. Maybe (probably) the critics who've spent their lives studying film and politics and the flirtation and courtship between the two are right. Maybe *FMJ* is antiwar. But let me (with my last few breaths before the finish) again say that I don't think so.

Stanley Kubrick and my old man both loved a story. One of the first orders of business for Kubrick while getting ready to begin work on *Full Metal Jacket* was to ask Michael Herr for "a good Vietnam story," something with a movie in it. Even if he hated war, he loved tale-telling more. Without violence, that permanent and ubiquitous human expression, there could be no truly terrifying cinema. Even if he wasn't a futurist, Kubrick certainly played to that philosophy well. I'm convinced that he wanted to shock, frighten, captivate, and wound people. A lot of war movies, in Kubrick's mind, don't do that (including his first picture *Paths of Glory*, which Kubrick disliked enough to discount it as a war movie entirely).

Stanley Kubrick (if we must reduce him to a pity aphorism) would've believed something along the lines of "Truth Hurts." While fictionalizing war and framing it for his own aesthetic purposes, he maintains the zany, conflicting, and sometimes-hilarious dynamics of humans doing human things, even if those things are horrific. He refused to shrink from his vision. *Full Metal Jacket* is an anti-war-movie-movie.

For those who would maintain the old philosophy that it's antiwar, I'd just say this: It's not.

WORKS CONSULTED

Gengaro, Christine Lee. *Listening to Stanley Kubrick.* Scarecrow Press, 2013. Maryland. Paper.

Hasford, Gustav. *The Short-Timers.* Bantam, 1989. New York. Paper.

Hill, Rodney and Phillips, Gene D. *Great Filmmakers: The Encyclopedia of Stanley Kubrick.* Checkmark Books, 2002. New York. Paper.

Herr, Michael. *Dispatches.* Knopf, 1977. New York. Paper.

Herr, Michael. *Kubrick.* Grove Press, 2000. New York. Paper.

Nelson, Maggie. *The Art of Cruelty.* Norton, 2011. New York. Paper.

Rughani, Pratap. "Kubrick's Lens: Dispatches from the Edge." *Stanley Kubrick: New Perspectives* (ed. Ljujic, Kramer, and Daniels). Black Dog Publishing. UK. Paper.

DO YOU SUCK DICKS?

I am my father's son. This comes with anatomy and gear—some of it hangs off me, some of it I carry in a rucksack of recollection and ill-timed resemblance to the old man. I go out for beers as all the men in my family have always done, except for my dad, the token teetotaler. In this, my drinking, I don't worry about becoming him. But I can't relax too much, can I? It's never an impossibility that heredity will take over. I think I have to *hit the head*, as the Parris Island crew might say; see, I'm re-becoming a Full Metal Man as we speak. I don't know how long this will last.

Of course, I find myself in the men's room; why wouldn't I? I have a cock, I have balls. I am a man. If I were chasing after pussy like a man ought to do, I'd kick open the ladies' room door and catch old Mary Jane Rottencrotch with her purdy pink panties around her ankles and I'd lust-fuck her, but I'm just here to take a pee. Standing up, admiring the shadow of my dick across the tile by the toilet.

*

I read what I've written in my father's voice and it does not compute. He didn't talk like that; those are my words as I try to imagine him. I must read them in my own voice. Frighten or disgust myself. Have a conversation. Why did I make the words up in paragraph one? What am I thinking about? There's a process of discovery and self-disclosure in this, an excavation of an archaeological self. Horseshit, it's a parody. Maybe not exactly, but it's a hyperbolic caricature of the gender roles I was raised with. Closer to true; I'm getting warmer.

*

Hartman is mocking Gomer Pyle, who has repeatedly fallen off the log obstacle he's trying to climb. He is muddy and panting. Hartman bellows:

I bet you could drag ass up there for some pussy, isn't that right?"

Sir, yes sir.

I don't know how old I was when it happened, but it did: I pinched a woman's butt in the luggage department at Sears. My old man was chasing me and he saw it happen in slow motion. The woman wheeled around and looked right over me. She saw Pop and began to unthroat a scream. Frantically, he pointed down: "*Look*," he said with his body, "*Boy. Little. Mistake.*" The woman looked down and all was forgiven. My big brown eyes and my shock of curly blond hair absolved me.

"Oh! What an adorable little girl," the woman said.

Dad scooped me up in his arms and made haste to find my mother. She was looking at dishes, let us say. Or a vacuum. Perhaps something pink. Once he found Mom, Dad handed me off to her.

"Take him and go get his fuckin' hair cut."

Dad wasn't afraid of me being treated like a girl. He was afraid of being the father of a feminine boy. Self-interest first. Always. A military man who believed in dying for one's brothers could simultaneously be a superficial and pride-driven solipsist. He could be everything, but somehow, not what he wanted. I probably knew that at a young age. I probably knew I would never be the son of a suicide father, too. What will we know in the morning, us unroyal we?

*

When I get to high school my father gives me dating advice:

"Right now, girls are like bowling balls. You pick 'em up, finger 'em, and throw 'em in the gutter."

I laugh. I am still laughing. Girls are like nothing else. Joke's on you, Pop.

*

I get to college, the first time. My father gives me dating advice:

"Find one you like and stick with her. They'll all make you fuckin' crazy."

Listen hard enough and you'll hear my father's voice. Which side of his mouth do you listen to?

This is what it's like to be me.

*

I want to tell you I was looking in the mirror and all of a sudden I saw someone else, or that my reflection startled me into some deep reverie. But I walked into the bathroom of a bar on Boylston and I pissed in the urinal, washed my hands without soap, dried them on my jeans, and I left. It was late and I was tanked. I emptied my bladder. I, me, the agent of this entire anticlimax.

What trips the trigger is this: a person with shoulders broad like mine and an Adam's apple is walking into the ladies' room.

"We're over here man," I say.

The person does not stop. The person opens the door.

"Dude, that's the chicks', ours is right here."

I am raising my voice now, pointing, gesticulating.

"Dude," I say again.

The person is a half-body now. Halfway in, halfway out. Liminal. They turn their head.

"I'm trans, I pee sitting down. In the girls' room. Fuck off."

The person walking into the ladies' room has become me pinching some lady's ass. As a child, I did what felt natural even though it was not appropriate to the adults. The person is me, though they and I are both not me. We are going to revisit my duality. We are going to be both of me, committing a crime of reflex. I plead guilty twice. For me, one crime was groping a stranger. For me, it is also a crime to see what someone looks like but not who that person is.

We both, the person and I, were mistaken for someone else in a way, but I had my father to protect me in a way. The person had themself. Who am I more grateful to? Who should I admire? Must I choose, as my father did? As the person does?

When it came to fighting, Dad taught me this: If you can walk away, walk. If you can talk your way out of it, talk. If you have to fight, win.

My father and his simple complexities. If he ever understood himself, I'd love to know what he knew.

*

Did I stop for a moment to feel like an asshole? Did I rebuke myself for presumptuousness? Did I? Or did I just shrug and sigh and dismiss the episode as the type of awkward mishap that could only happen today? Did any of this happen or am I remembering in allegory? A parable can impregnate our memory, I'm sure. We are at the end, where the arrow has landed; of course we want to know from whence it was fired.

I go to another bar in another town on a different night of the same life and I use the facilities there. On the doors to each restroom are spray-painted letters: Dudes, etc., Ladies, etc.

Simple fix.

Either, Or, Unless. Even the Lusthog squad lived by this. Either it's peacetime or its go-time. Unless we're just trembling behind our rifles or crying in our bunks. Then it's some weird otherness. That otherness is the lion's share of the time we spend in this world. Pee in the wrong room. Fuck it. Maybe it's the right one.

*

My old man wouldn't know how to walk through a world where people aren't male or female. Some people are trans— mismatched to the bodies they got after nine months of boot camp in the womb, sailors in the Air Force—other people are both or neither, conscientious objectors with automatic weapons. For some people, it depends on the day or their serotonin level. For some people, there is no such thing as gender and there is no reason for cooperative sex acts. We could continue *ad infinitum.*

When Pop was alive, there were two genders. Two you could be in public, anyway.

Dad's prejudice came easily because there were only two orientations when he was alive: straight or gay. No polyamorous pansexual dominant/submissives. No sapiosexuality. You were either a man or a woman. You were straight or you were wrong.

*

Like Hartman says of the Marine Corps, marginal genders or sexual expressions are forever. If anyone should've sympathized with confliction, wasn't it my father? Who among us could be more anxious to look one way while being another? What was I going to do with this template—I knew or at least wanted to think about knowing. But we age into and out of ourselves. There's always going to be my father. He'll be in the archives of some video library of the soul, or some other abstruse shit like that. He'll be everywhere, like the enemy. But will he be the enemy? Anybody's guess.

Lisa calls to tell me her daughter isn't her daughter anymore, but she doesn't have an extra son now, either. "*Do I understand,*" she asks. "*Do I get what she's saying,*" she asks. My partner, whom I've promised to stand by, calls to tell me her youngest child is nonbinary. But she doesn't define that. Can't. Will try later. Promises. Promises me, promises the child. God bless the child. God help the child. God—

*

Pop is parked in front of the TV again. This is predictable. What comes from the tube and the concave glass is predictable too: *Full Metal Jacket.*

[Hartman to a Private] Do you suck cock?

[Private Anyone Who Doesn't Wish to Die on the Deck at Hartman's Feet] Sir, no sir!

[Hartman] Bullshit! I bet you could polish a pecker to a high shine without using your hands!

"Janet," Dad says.

"Yes?"

"What do we do if the boy turns out to be gay?"

[Hartman to Cowboy] Do you fuck boys?

[Cowboy] Sir, no sir!

[Hartman] Are you a buttfucker?

[Cowboy] Sir, no sir!

[Hartman] I bet you'd hump a fella from behind without even telling him he's pretty. I don't trust you, I'll be watching.

*

It was mandatory for all five-year-old children in 1988 to know how to skip before they were in kindergarten. Skipping, my old man told me, was a lot like walking only you jumped between each step, and before you jumped you made sure the other foot was ready to step, and the first foot that stepped would then jump, and then—

It should be clear by now that my father was a fat man. It should also be clear that he was impatient and inarticulate. He was also a shit-awful teacher. He went on trying to explain skipping to me using mixed metaphors and saying something about imagining a retarded flamingo square dancing with a hula hoop. Nah, I'm just fucking with you. He tried for about five minutes to scare me into skipping by yelling at me and slapping my palms with his palms, hard.

"Fuck this noise, only faggots skip anyway."

*

The number of words above this line was supposed to be 1138.

*

I am eighteen years old. Rail thin and I don't need to shave half as often as I do. I trim the hair on my belly into a straight line, a stairway to heaven, I call it. I have not been laid yet, but I'm used to getting girls on account of my looks. I'm very pretty and I like to shop. Black belt and brown shoes? Sinful. A dress shirt anything less than crisply starched and tucked in without any blousing at all? Would never happen. Not to me.

My mother calls me her metrosexual beauty queen. My father just calls me Boy, as if to remind me that I am.

"Look at these abs," I say, flexing my runner's stomach and marveling at the definition of the muscles. A thousand sit-ups a day are paying off. "I'm getting fuckin' ripped." I say something about modeling for Abercrombie—something about how windswept and sun kissed and forever young the models in the catalog were. And how there were always girls with their tits out and how if I were one of the male bodies that made it into the catalog, I'd get to be there for that.

"I can get you a photo session," Dad says. "I know a guy."

He is looking at me in some new way. Like he's really seeing me standing there, topless, and full of myself.

"That'd be cool," I say. "Who do you know?"

"There's a guy named Phillip who's gotten more people into pro modeling than any other—"

I laugh harder than I want to or should.

"You don't know that guy, you just saw his ad on the internet. Dude's a joke. One of the girls in my speech class models. She can probably hook me up."

"Don't you think you'd be running the risk of—"

"Rejection? Sure. But look at these abs, man. C'mon. I'm a miracle of modern masculinity."

Did I really say that? Does it matter? I was brutally shy and secretly felt ugly every day. Does that matter? Is it germane?

"God's gift to women and all that crap," Mom says. She is smiling. "God's gift to me, anyway." She pats my butt because she knows I hate it. Because she knows she can get away with it.

"I'm just concerned that you're risking a life that will lead you away."

"Away from where?" Mom asks.

"Away from home?" I say.

"Away from the church," Dad says. "Don't you think this modeling business would lead you astray?"

"Jesus, Jeffrey," Mom says.

I am laughing again. I shouldn't be laughing. Never should've started. I am a sniper taking out little bits of Dad with every snort and knee slap.

"You're afraid I'm going to be gay if I'm a model. That's it, isn't it?"

"Andrew Philip, that's enough. I do not appreciate—"

"You're scared I'm gonna get a boyfriend if I pose for Abercrombie. That I'll bring home some fairy and you'll have to—"

"Motherfucker, I offer to help you and you mock me with queer jokes. You're lucky your mother is alive and my dick still works. Otherwise, Boy—"

Otherwise Boy. That's my superhero name. My mother gave it to me after the old man died. Not literally. Not out loud. But we share a silent understanding that everything we do, say, share, think, feel, expect, are amazed by, fall in love with, or crack up laughing at is, to some degree, an otherwise. I am Andy, whose friends call him Cowboy. I am Andrew, whose friends call him Captain Pabst's first mate. I am,

211

otherwise, Boy. Ma still calls me Baby Boy. Sometimes *My* Baby Boy, sometimes *Little* Boy. Sometimes an amalgamation of the two. Fuck. It's been too long since I was coarse. I'm feeling baby's-bottom-naked and yet not nearly as smooth. Mama tucks me into bed when I sleep on the couch upstairs. She actually says *tuck, tuck, tuck* as she light fingers the blanket around my big body. Then she blesses me with the benediction we both know by rote.

"May the Lord bless you and keep you. May the Lord lift up His countenance upon you and be gracious unto you. May the Lord look upon you with favor and give you His peace."

She baptizes me without water but in the name of God and with the sign of the cross on my forehead. Whatever God and Daddy are doing tonight, Mama has my six.

She has never admitted to wondering if God is a She. Neither have I. There is theology on this. Theology that states the love God has for the mortal platoon of Gomer Pyle's, which is humanity, is more maternal than fatherly. But Mama doesn't read much that isn't a mystery novel or historical fiction about the Holocaust. She's usually content to watch movies. She usually lets me pick. Mama only rarely breaks character.

*

"Janet," Dad says.

"Yes?"

"What do we do if the boy turns out to be gay?"

I've kept it a secret from you, how my mother answers this. Her reply is one of the weaknesses of writing nonfiction, and yet one of the biggest strengths of living it. Mom's reply was natural and there was no dramatic pause. To her, it was an annoyance that she even had to say anything on the topic.

"We'll love him."

That's what she said.

*

I don't want to give you the impression that my father was trapped in time forever. He grew a little.

Pop got me my bellboy job, the one I've had for sixteen years as of this keystroke. He was still working full-time at the Post Office, but part-time as a third shift security officer at the hotel. Our night auditor, the man who worked the front desk overnight and therefore knew my old man pretty well, was gay. Very. Quite. Unapologetically. Gay.

His name was Michael, and he thought my dad was cute.

"He's absolutely goddamn cuddly!"

"He's also a homophobe," I'd remind Michael.

"Everybody is until they learn a thing or three."

We'd giggle and Mike would pretend to kiss the idea of my father.

One night, at home, Dad nudged me and said:

"You know Michael calls me Shnuckums?"

"No, but that's fucking priceless."

"I call him Loverboy."

Oh, reader. How do I explain the depth and girth of my emotion at this? Two men, both tall, thick, and bald, invoking pet names at the workplace. One sincere. The other, who could say? Maybe my Pops wasn't such a hillbilly after all.

In any event, they gave each other platoon names. They were playacting in the movie for which they were cast. It wasn't *Full Metal Jacket*; there wasn't room for a suddenly-tolerant-of-faggots drill sergeant in this one. There were only roles for odd humans.

*

Both Michael and my father committed suicide. I would never make this shit up.

*

The total number of words above this line is not 1138 multiplied by two. It's some exponent or other. Some base. The total number of words above this line is an outcome.

*

Fast-forwarding seems cheap, like it's cheating—it feels something like inviting you over to watch a movie but only showing you the parts I think are valuable. And yet it's a kindness, believe me, to skip over the tedium and contradictions, the setbacks and regressions that were symptomatic of any kind of maturation in my family. Let us press play on November 8, 2016.

Mom and I are together at The Heavy Anchor, our favorite bar in St. Louis. The front room is a long bar with a spacious dartboard corner and a videogame/reading corner bookending the front door. This room is separated from the other side, the music venue, by a garage door on which there is a graffiti-style narwhal having a kung fu sparring session with a bright orange octopus. There are sailboats of varying sizes with captains smoking joints and who have mermaid harems attending to them. The garage door is, however, open. Tonight the entire place is a watch party for the presumptive coronation of Hillary Rodham Clinton.

"She's not just a woman," Mom says. "She's tough. She knows how to handle herself. We're not all housewives anymore."

"Cheers," I say.

Mom clinks her glass of Diet Coke to my tallboy of Pabst.

"What do you think Dad would do?" I say.

"About what?" The election, of course. I want to hear my mother tell me she thinks Pop would support a female candidate, and then see if she can make me believe it. "He'd have voted for Hillary. Trump's rich, your dad wouldn't have trusted him."

"HRC is loaded too, though."

"Yeah, but your dad liked Slick Willy. When Hillary wins, Slick Willy gets to be The First Man. Your dad would love that."

She's right, although I still can't see Dad punching the ballot for Hillary.

But he doesn't get a vote. Mom's close-cropped hair is freshly trimmed and she looks almost like a little girl.

"Jan, I love your hair," our sort-of-buddy Dave says in passing. "You look like my favorite lesbian aunt."

"Not all dykes have short hair, asshole," someone we don't know responds. "Look at me: hair down to my ass and I'm the biggest queer in the room."

This person is, indeed, quite large. A playful debate about who can out-gay everyone else ensues. At the forefront is Danny, a Guatemalan dude with a baby face and whose taste in men is as eclectic as my taste in music.

"I'd go out with Andy," Danny says. He stands on a barstool, drunker than usual for this time of night, and bellows it again. "I'd go out with Andy!" He points at me and blows me a kiss. "But I'd also go out with Mama Jan!"

Never mind the election. What would my father think of this; his wife in a gay-friendly bar, watching her son get drunk and Donald Trump get elected President?

Donald Trump. He Who Dismantles The Jovial Vibe. By the night's end, Mom and Danny are in one another's arms, sobbing. Mom is baffled. Danny is terrified. He is homosexual and has brown skin; Trump hates him. Same-sex marriage is a ballot issue coming in Missouri. Danny doesn't want to get married, but what about people who do?

"Love is love," Mom murmurs, like a prayer. She strokes Danny's hair like she once did mine when I was sick and a child.

The self-proclaimed biggest queer in the room joins the cuddling wounded. Dave, who's been forgiven for his reckless mouth, and Jodie who co-owns the bar get in there, too. I stand outside the circle, crying a little myself. There is a lifetime of forward in front of me, and yet my country—and my father's—is moving back.

*

We fast-forward again, this time to this afternoon. Trump is tweeting his daily idiocies and Mom is reading the news on her tablet.

"This motherfucker," she says. "He's not right. In the head, I mean."

"Think he's a Section 8?"

"Ooo-rah," she says. "He can't hack it."

"Ignore him for a while, Ma. Let's watch a movie."

"I'm not your father, I can't be distracted that easy. This man is crazy."

"Could you be distracted by dark chocolate and *Steel Magnolias?*"

"You hate that movie."

Not today I don't, Ma. Really, I don't.

*

But can I rewind, now, to share something with you?

My mother in bars; that's a story with an arc. Two days after Pop shot himself, Mom wandered over to Super's Bungalow with me. I had developed a superhuman tolerance for alcohol that night, so I don't remember getting drunk. However, everybody but mom and I did. An Asian woman with good intentions (her name escapes me) kept leaning over Mom and telling her, in broken slurs, "everything's gone be find." Mom smiled, nodded. She did not cry once.

Fast forward four years and change:

Super Bowl, 2011. Dad's favorite team, the Green Bay Packers, win their first title in years. Mom and I are in a casino sports bar; I'm shitfaced, she's driving us home. She high-fives some strangers and asks me if I'd like some of her soda. She never stops smiling, even as I vomit in a cement corner of the parking garage.

*

Then Election Night, the story you know.

*

Shortly after a return trip to Super's Bungalow, which is a barbecue joint now.

An old man named Fred, who I've talked baseball with for years, outs himself as a Trumper.

"He's going to be great," Fred says. "That nigger Obama was a disaster. And Hillary oughtta be in jail."

"For what?" Mom says.

"All them emails and shit. C'mon, you watch the news."

"I do. And I read. And I think Trump is a bully, a crook, and he's sucking Putin's dick."

"You shouldn't care about that. All you snowflakes want two fags to be able to do whatever they want."

"You're goddamn right." Mom is standing now, pushing against my body, which has rather stupidly moved between her and Fred. "I think Trump and Putin should be able to get married if they want. But he's got no call being—"

"Shut up, woman, you're full of shit."

Mom is ready to brawl. I do not notice myself shove her, just slightly, away from me. I do not notice myself turning, becoming taller than I am. I do notice the beer in my glass leaving it. I notice Fred's eyes widening and his stool tipping backward. I don't hear anything until I hear my mother whispering, "Okay, okay, okay. It's over. It's over."

"I'm sorry," I hear myself say. "Fred, you have a big fucking mouth."

"Yeah. That I do."

Mom and I descend the concrete stairs and I'm shaking with shame and rage. She is rubbing my back with her left hand and holding a six-pack of beer in her right.

"I paid our tab," she says. "I tipped a little extra."

"Ma?"

"I know."

Knowing without my saying. This is the story of my life with Madre. I don't have to explain why I love or hate or mourn or miss my father to her. I have to explain it to myself, which is harder. I try less with me. That's why I have you.

*

The number of words in this section was 1138. It's not anymore.

I'm sorry Pop. I thought I could finesse one more of your number into this thing. I couldn't.

Listen: I could've Dad. I didn't.

Etc.

SOME KIND OF SICK JOKE?

I was saying something about Jung and — Think back to Joker's response to being questioned about having Born to Kill written on his helmet. Is it a joke? Some sick communist insurrectionist rhetorical flourish? No. It's a nod to Carl Jung and man's two natures. Thirty-plus years later, that's still Joker's explanation; it's public record, permanent. But ponder this: do we underestimate humankind if we agree with that conventional wisdom? If we settle for duality? What happens if, instead, we invest humankind with triplicity, suggest every individual is a trinity?

I'm Ok—You're Ok, the seminal work of transactional analysis by Thomas A. Harris, came out in 1967; it is, therefore, fair to call it Vietnam-era psychology. In the book, Dr. Harris identifies three individuations present in each of us. Each seems either neo or post-Freudian, as each deals with internalized rules and stimuli, emotional impulses, and our ability or inability to cope therewith. I doubt my old man ever read it. The cover of his copy is pristine. The pages are yellowed evenly, there's no break in the spine. No marginalia. This is to say: the book tells on him in more ways than one; because even though he likely never read it, it is without a doubt his psychological snapshot, just as *Full Metal Jacket* is his biopic.

*

Individuation One:

"The parent is a huge collection of recordings in the brain of unquestioned or imposed external events perceived by a person in his early years . . ."

Outside the jargon of the head-shrinker, this persona is the embodiment of what we internalize from our upbringing: don't put your elbows on the table, it's okay to wipe your nose on your sleeve, don't raise your voice to your mother, vote on more than one issue, driving the speed limit is going too slow, sex before marriage is a sin but sins are meant to be forgiven. Men are the heads of the household. Women are silent. Soldiers, policemen, firefighters, and your father are doing what's right. Always. As Dr. Harris says: "Much Parent data in current living appears in the how-to category: how to hit a nail, how to make a bed . . . how to dress a Christmas tree . . . A person whose early instructions were accompanied by stern intensity may . . . [have] developed a compulsion to do it "this way" and no other." This was the case with my father; do it one way, do it Kubrick's way, do it 7.62: full metal jacket.

The book defines four life positions: I'm Not Ok, You're Ok; I'm Not Ok, You're Not OK; I'm Ok, You're Not Ok; I'm Ok, You're Ok. The Parent places us initially, in position number one. This is to say, we all begin at the beginning. We are taught to cower before authority. We are small, the Parent is large; we are dependent, the Parent provides; we are weak, the Parent is strong. We are in a world of shit, the Parent is the world. This position is universal, the book says; we're all Not Ok as infants and toddlers. We can become Ok, the book says. Or we can not

The Parent, Dr. Harris writes, isn't limited to our biological parents. TV can be a Parent extension; if our parents condone violent programming, it's like receiving a double blessing. Harris concludes that someone exposed to this twinning of exposure and endorsement:

". . . assumes permission to be violent provided he collects the required amount of injustices."

Required amount of injustices: eight weeks on Parris Island.

Required amount of injustices: fifty-two years of being Jeffrey Michael Smart.

Full Metal Jacket gave both Pyle and my father the permission they needed.

I don't blame the film; Pyle was a character—his permission was written by Stanley Kubrick, Gustav Hasford, and Michael Herr.

I blame my father. He had a choice. He could've turned the movie off, stopped the recording and replaying of all that internalized agony.

I blame my father's parents, and maybe their parents.

I blame everyone, everywhere, all the time.

I blame myself.

I can't blame the Parent structure. That one is only exterior stimuli.

*

Individuation Two:

The Child is our emotional cache from that time: the fear, the reluctance to confront authority, the impulse to cry when angry, the reflex to strike ourselves in the head and face when we are too flustered to do anything else. The Child contains our coping dysfunctions and our insecurities; it holds, too, our tattered happiness.

When I was in my early teens and needed service hours for school, my old man and I joined a group at our church called The Carpenters' Workshop, where anybody in the congregation who was even a little bit handy volunteered to do household projects for parishioners. My first one was tearing the roof off my first-grade teacher's house. It was a thousand degrees on the tarpaper, and we didn't start until the sun was high. We slipped, we swore, we sweat like it was the Ia Drang Valley. But we didn't quit.

Afterward, Ms. Mangles drank a steinie bottle of Budweiser and beheld our work. Her hair was the same bob cut it was when I was six, her glasses the same stained glass looking frames with their bifocal demarcations. I wondered if she still spit when she talked, but I was already drenched and it wouldn't have mattered. My days in the front row of her classroom were over and I had no spelling book to repurpose as an umbrella.

"Wow, boys, you really put your backs into it. When can you come back and start on the new one?"

Everyone was quiet. Nobody wanted to be the first one to say "tomorrow," but it was equally distasteful to say, "we need a break." I don't remember who spoke first but there it was:

"We could probably get back at it in the morning."

"Yeah," Dad seconded. "I took two days off."

He looked at me. His eyes said: "Stay home and sleep if you want."

"It's August," I said. "I'm off for two more weeks. I'll be here."

We stopped for gas and Cokes on the way home. I pounded a twenty-ounce bottle and started back for another.

"I brought you a second," Dad called after me. "Figured that'd happen."

"Thanks."

"You're welcome. Did a man's day of work today. You were more balls than that lazy fuck Pat Logan. It was like he'd never seen a hammer or shovel before. He took more breaks than anybody, including you."

"We weren't there to take breaks. We were there to get something done."

"My boy," Pop said. He smiled and patted my head. "I'm proud of you."

*

I can't tell you how it felt to hear those words—the euphoric juvenilia, I guess I'd call it, that accompanied any praise from my father. But I can tell you every time I sit down in the car after a long day of work, I feel it again, exactly as it was in that instant. Then it fades into a recollection of Dad's face that day, of the sheen of perspiration on his bald head, the open cuts on his forearms. I am back in his car, for a moment, because every steering wheel looks like ours did. See: even as an Adult, I am still my father's Child.

This is how we function, according to *I'm Ok—You're Ok*. Our Child gets a glimpse or whiff of something that jars loose a sensation from youth and recreates that sensation. It's only after a moment, or even a few days, that we remember what made us feel that way in the first place. Be it adulation or despondency, that's how the Child works.

What's key then is knowing which mixture thereof constitutes our Child, and how the third structure, the Adult, manages it.

*

Individuation Three:

The Adult is, like Freud's Ego, the mature mediator in all of us. He's the offspring of the Parent and the Child and can even have some of the same incestuous consequences. The Adult is maladapted if he holds onto either too much of the Parent's authoritarian sway or the Child's emotionality. The Adult is supposed to be a multitasking filter structure: retain old precepts that work, chuck the rest and adopt your own attitudes; acknowledge and appreciate healthy expressions of emotion and appropriate times and doses, sublimate the remainder. Function, adapt, thrive.

As much as *Full Metal Jacket* is a male movie, *I'm Ok, You're Ok* is a book about manhood.

In the cinescape of *FMJ*, it's tidy but true to label Hartman (Parent), Pyle (Child) and Joker (Adult). The *I'm Ok—You're Ok* trifecta. Given Pop's intoxication with the film, these characters and their corresponding structures became his identity. As Dr. Harris tells us, the consequences of this are almost inevitably dire.

"Once finalized, the Child stays in his chosen position and it governs everything he does . . . People do not shift back and forth," Harris writes. In *FMJ*, Pyle gets stuck in Not Ok; we can argue, as sympathetic sots, that this is understandable. It matters not. What matters is that Pyle is perpetually mired in an emotionally reactive state of victimization—when in league with Pyle, my father was in the same Child state. This Child, constantly reacting negatively and quaking before others, tries to drag down the Adult.

Dr. Harris points to the condition "traumatic neurosis," in which Child, Parent, and Adult are bombarded with this negativity at once. "These people may . . . engage in an elaborate wish-life of *if I* and *when I*. Another person's script may call for behavior that is provoking to the point where others turn on him." My father's escapism and asinine behaviors indicate that even in neurotic manifestations he was a man of multiples.

Any given afternoon he could be the forehead-kissing father who was sorry to go to work. He could be the jolly fat man who took his son to White Castle for hillbilly brunch every other Sunday. Or he could be the farting, belching, sexist who delighted in the idea that his memoir would one day be titled Men Are Pigs. Or, instead of interacting with anyone, he could be the hermit in the basement playing Age of Empires. He could conquer virtual worlds but never master his selves.

And, as I theorized, was ultimately a triplicate:

"The ultimate resolution of this position is . . . suicide."

Can I indulge in intentional fallacy and say Stanley Kubrick knew this? That he made a Vietnam movie using Vietnam-era theory and let it seduce men of a Vietnam age? I can't. I can only point to the final scene of the first act of *Full Metal Jacket*.

Joker, Pyle, and Hartman, are all in one room, alone. This is the only time this happens. The distress, the resentment, the quasi-Freudian, Jungian, Thomas-Harrisan thing is intact.

My father, for once, is intact.

Joker, the Adult, tries to reason with Pyle:

Take it easy, Leonard.

Hartman, the Parent, does the only thing he knows:

He screams. What the fuck is wrong with you? Are you having daddy issues? Did somebody hurt your feelings? Drop the fucking gun before I fuck you up!

Pyle fulfills the prophecy of scriptwriting and psychobabble. Gun down Hartman, menace Joker, turn the gun on yourself.

Born to Kill. Just like my dad.

*

The gaping hole in this logic is that Joker is still alive. The Adult survives. This is what makes *Full Metal Jacket* fiction. Joker's character is based on J.T. Davis, the first confirmed American casualty in Vietnam. It is history as only Kubrick could write it: first to die, alive at the end. Although, even in the structures of transactional analysis, Joker proves our theorem:

Born to Kill on your helmet: Parent.

Peace button: Child.

Lonely Marine under all of it: Adult.

Semper Fi, Do or Die, Gung Ho. Gung Ho. Gung Ho.

Some Thoughts on the Death of a Drill Instructor

Ronald Lee Ermey was born in Emporia, Kansas on the twenty-fourth of March 1944. His folks were called John and Betty. His wife, whom he married in 1975, is named Nila. Thus spoke Wikipedia. It doesn't give me much satisfaction to know that the man who played Gunnery Sergeant Hartman was a farm boy from the heartland, or that he got arrested twice in Washington state and enlisted in the military because it was a better deal than prison.

It doesn't make me feel warm and fuzzy to think about the four kids the internet tells me he has; in fact, with the belly full of resentment I have toward Hartman, I cringe a little to think about Ermey as a dad. Maybe I'm having trouble with him the way I started to with Vincent D'Onofrio—I can't separate him from the one role I remember best. I liked Ermey in *Se7en*, with Morgan Freeman and Brad Pitt, too. Come to think of it, he was in *Mississippi Burning*, as well. Just like my Pops: a whole body of work but I only give him credit for one role.

He took more of Hartman with him than Vince took Gomer Pyle, and maybe that's my problem. Ermey was at home in the awfulness of *Full Metal Jacket*. He had that authority in his voice that made you believe that *he believed* everything he was saying. There's a common misconception in the world that about ninety percent of Hartman's lines were adlibbed by R. Lee Ermey; from what I've read it was less than a third, though Kubrick did make edits where he thought it necessary. Dad thought that was true—that we were watching R. Lee Ermey remember his glory days and revert to the badass D.I. who got shit done. I believed it too because I believed in my father.

And R. Lee Ermey took the name "Gunny Lee" in later life, hosting shows on cable about military history and how to shoot heavy artillery as a civilian. Or some shit like that; I never watched.

I know a few things about the man's life. Do I want to learn any more? I can't say that I do. That's today's answer. I realize that when I started writing this book I wanted to know everything about Ermey, Vince, Kubrick, *Full Metal Jacket*, and my dad. But today I'm just a little sad that an old man died from pneumonia in a California ICU. I kind of wish he'd have lived to be a cute old fella in a wheelchair, one of those dotards who don't really know what's going on anymore but who wear hats that say "*(Insert Armed Conflict Here) Veteran*" and people go up and thank them. I kind of wish he'd lived into his diaper days.

See? The old vitriol comes back just fast. So too it is with my dad—I love him, I hate him, I miss him, I wish I could forget him. Wishing to forget. That's what I should call my incomplete, unauthorized, and utterly biased biography of R.

Lee Ermey. I wish I could forget him the way I'm forgetting the sound of my father's voice (have I cried about that already in here?). I wish I could forget all the lines I quote from *Full Metal Jacket* and the way I cock my shoulders like a drill sergeant when I'm pissed off. I wish I could forget to be pissed off sometimes.

*

Here are the facts: R. Lee Ermey is dead and his funeral is going to be at Arlington National Cemetery. He'll get the same colors draped on his GI coffin that my father did. He'll have the same twenty-one-gun salute, the same taps. But he won't have the same bagpiper Dad did, and he won't have my mother in her wrinkled dress clothes from J.C. Penney. My drunk uncle's forearm won't be across my chest as I sob in the heat and reach for the casket. Not at this funeral. Hartman once told us: Marines die because it's what we do. I can't help but wonder if, at seventy-four, Gunny Lee still bought that line. Let's say he did. Fuck it. Drive on.

Here are the facts, too: I cried at work when Lisa called to tell me about Gunny Lee's passing. I didn't cry like Pyle, wailing in his bunk. But I did cry. Gunny kept me tethered to my father. With him in the world, I could at least know Dad's ego ideal still existed. Complications from respiratory distress cut the tether. It's stupid to mourn for a stranger, I'm told. But R. Lee Ermey was family.

PICKING UP MY COVER

If I were a grunt, what would I write on my helmet?

*

Most marines in *Full Metal Jacket* had inscriptions on their headgear. Some of them were badges of identity—who they were before they were killers, stalkers, insomniacs, pranksters, or literary devices. Others are responses to the selves these warriors had assumed. What any of these men wrote on his helmet was a response to their version of *all this.*

Animal Mother had this partial quote that Robert Oppenheimer had cribbed from the Bhagavad-Gita:

"I Am Become Death."

Another grunt had this whistling-in-the-dark affirmation:

"I'm Hard."

Cowboy had a confederate flag with a photo of either Jefferson Davis, Buddy Holly, or Abraham Lincoln in the center. It depends on whose opinion you trust.

Some of the guys had crosses pinned or otherwise affixed to their helmets. Pretty much everyone had a water bottle full of who-can-say.

*

If I were a grunt, then, what would my helmet say? How would I respond to *all this*: writing about mental illness and suicide, living and reliving my younger days with Dad, addressing film and how it works, empathy and how it fails, who my mother and I have become in relation to one another. All this. *All this.*

This is where my life isn't like *Full Metal Jacket* at all. See, I can change helmets whenever I want to. Sometimes, whether I know it or not, one helmet falls off or gets blown up and then another just lands on me, some strange weight that doesn't register as to what it is.

*

The day Pop shot himself, I ended up wearing a helmet that was three sizes too big and was obviously straight from the PX. On it, I managed to scrawl:

"Ain't No Fortunate Son," after the Creedence Clearwater Revival song. I'd been a good son to a bad father, I reckoned, and there was nothing fortunate about my circumstances. I was timid at first about how angry I was, but that went away and I kept darkening and re-darkening the letters on my helmet. Ain't no fortunate sons here. Sir, negative sir. I didn't want to be using militaristic images and the persona of *Full Metal Jacket*, but my instinct took me there.

*

A few hours after Dad was buried, Mom and I went back to the cemetery to find his gravesite. I wore that same black felt 10x Stetson I wore to bull rides and to commit adultery. Just inside the hat band I put a piece of torn notebook paper that read "Cowboy Up." I took the hat off out of respect for a woman who, while consoling us, told us her three-year-old son was buried just rows behind my old man. His name was Nick. Turns out the hotel chain I work for hosted a Mickey Mouse themed party for him before he died. He was too sick to travel. Too close to death.

*

Right now, I'd probably write something quasi-poetic:
"I Am Become the Screaming Diminuendo"
Or
"Death Where Is Thy Air Support?"
Or

"What's The Worst That Could Happen?"

It's close to peacetime around me right now. I've had Thai food and a cup of coffee, it's fifty-something degrees out, and spring training games are on TV. I can be a little lax, a little flippant with my coat of arms.

*

I'm trying not to venture down the path of wondering what my dad's helmet would've said. I'm trying not to see the white flag of surrender pinned to it, below it the words:

"Bury Me Among My Brothers."

In his post-facto suicide note, Pop expressly asked to be buried where he was. "But whatever you decide will be find." A fucking typo in the denouement. Only my father could live like that.

*

Maybe that's what I'll write on tomorrow's helmet:

"Everything is Find."

It's true enough.

*

I wanted to leave you a long time ago. My guts are outside my body and there's not enough left to serve seconds. Picture me this way then:

I am one inch taller than Arliss Howard, who played Pvt. Cowboy. My beard is trimmed close to the cheeks, but flares into a homeless Viking face-mane in the mustache and chin. I am built like a guy who was much better at high-school football than I was. I am wearing my father's combat boots— the one's he was supposed to have turned in when he retired; there's nothing in any of the pockets of any of his old clothes that tells me why he kept these. It is 11:38pm, and I know this. I am wearing an invisible helmet that says:

"Fuck It, Drive On."

*

The Marine Corps motto is Semper Fi: Always Loyal.

The Missouri Army National Guard Motto is: Always Ready, Always There.

Dad was a better Marine than he was a guardsman. I can make that true because my helmet also says this:

"I Am Become Life, Reanimator of Worlds."

I have a whole armory of helmets, as a matter of fact:

I Am Become The Blue Horse after a dream I had and a series of paintings Franz Marc made and a book Mary Oliver wrote and a poem James Wright gave the world. I am become the blue horse—the only horse in this soldiered cowboy's Vietnam.

I Am Become The Alpha and The Omega because the story I tell begins and ends where I make it.

I Am Become My Own Blue Crayon, instead of the one I held in all the dreams I had for the first month after Dad died—where I was a toddler doodling the same thing over and over, always in blue: "I want my Daddy."

I Am Become: The Peace Sign, The War, The Battlefield, The Tank, The First Aid Kit, The Mess Tent, The Little Boy Waving At The Men Who Hold Their Guns Like Teddy Bears, The Wanderer, The Homebody, The Commandant, and The Corps.

I Am Become My Own Movie.

I Am Become The Leader of the Club That's Made For You And Me.

I Am Become.

In the name of my father and of his son, Amen.

In the name of this animal's mother, Amen.

Over and Out.

POSTSCRIPTS

Some of the intel in this manuscript is outdated now. Mainly I mean the references to the passage of time since my father's death. As I originally wrote this book, Dad's tenth anniversary had just passed. What happened in the years between then and now? Life, for as paradoxical as it sounds.

Building and producing a book is hard; there's more to it than writing the words. My old man likely would have predicted this from beyond the grave. He knew more than most that creating a story and getting it to fruition are two different things. There were mental health crises, extraneous family obligations, a global pandemic, the dissolution of a relationship, a near fistfight with a man on a bicycle, my uncle—a Vietnam veteran who vouches for *Full Metal Jacket* as an accurate depiction of, at the very least, boot camp—being diagnosed with cancer. Life. All of that is life. And its accretion led to this poetic factoid: this book was sent to the printer on the fifteenth anniversary of Dad's suicide, as if it were scripted that way. Forgive, then, the old references to "these last ten years" and so forth. The World Series reference that happened "this year" in real time but has now been several years ago. Forgive the dust on the movie reels, reader. I think you understand.

I believe also you will understand the repetitions you encounter herein. You meet the same characters, you see them perform the same actions, I beg you to focus on the same details of their outfits or expressions on multiple occasions. I want you in the living room with me or sitting in a secluded corner of the Webster University Library watching YouTube. You see these people, places, and things—these nouns which carry the vividness of verbs in my imagination—over and over again because I do. Immersion in the world of Kubrickian cinema drowned my father in self-harming empathetic bullshit. To emerge from that world of shit, to come through with a few scars and a fucked-up story, the same immersion was necessary. Roland Barthes would call this *mimesis*. Language rubbing at the seams of language. Reality and surreality creating a friction that calls into question the very essence of what a book, film, or story is.

I call it Basic Training. You've survived, graduated. Watch out for landmines.

Now, fall out.

You're dismissed.

ABOUT THE AUTHOR

Andy Smart earned his Master of Fine Arts degree from the Solstice Low-Residency Creative Writing Program at Pine Manor College. His poems have appeared, or are forthcoming in: *Lily Poetry Review, River Heron Review, Red Fez, Two-Thirds North, The American Journal of Poetry,* and elsewhere. His essays have been published in the anthologies *Show Me All Your Scars* (In Fact Books) and *Come Shining: Poems and Essays on Writing in a Dark Time* (Kelson Books), as well as: *Sleet Magazine, Moon City Review,* and *Glassworks* (forthcoming).

ABOUT THE PRESS

Unsolicited Press was founded in 2012 and is based out of Portland, Oregon. Many of its authors are award-winning and champions in their respective genres. The team works hard to publish voices that tackle difficult topics and bravely wade into the experimental.

Learn more at unsolicitedpress.com.